D0342875

Scientists Who Believe

Scientists Who Believe

edited by

Eric C. Barrett

and

David Fisher

MOODY PRESS
CHICAGO

© 1984 by
THE MOODY BIBLE INSTITUTE
OF CHICAGO

All Scripture quotations in this book, except those
noted otherwise, are from *The New American Standard Bible,* © 1960, 1962, 1963, 1968, 1971, 1972,
1973, 1975, and 1977 by The Lockman Foundation,
and are used by permission.

Library of Congress Cataloging in Publication Data

Main entry under title:

Scientists who believe.

   Selected scripts from the Radio Academy of Science,
Slavic Gospel Association.
   1. Scientists—Religious Life—Addresses, essays,
lectures. 2. Religion and science—1946 —Addresses,
essays, lectures. 3. Apologetics—20th century—Addresses, essays, lectures. I. Barrett, E. C. (Eric Charles)
II. Fisher, David, 1935-   . III. Radio Academy
of Science (Slavic Gospel Association)
BV4596.S35S38   1984   208'.85   83-25037

ISBN 0-8024-7634-1 (pbk.)

13 15 17 19 20 18 16 14

Printed in the United States of America

Contents

Foreword

In a wartime radio broadcast, Sir Winston Churchill once described Russia as "a riddle wrapped up in a mystery inside an enigma." While his description may be true in the political areas of life, it is certainly not true when it comes to matters that are spiritual. We *know* where the Russian government officially stands when it comes to religion! And there are many Christian believers in the free world who are concerned enough to do something about it.

The Radio Academy of Science represents one such effort to get the truth of the Bible past the Iron Curtain and into the minds and hearts of radio listeners. Prepared and produced by dedicated people who know both the Bible and contemporary science, these programs have had a profound effect not only on the common people, but also on the "intelligentsia" of the communist world.

The Dean of RADAS, Dr. Eric Barrett, is a remarkable man. I first met him in Bristol, England, where he serves as the respected Reader in Climatology and Remote Sensing at the University of Bristol. His work takes him to many corners of the world; he is recognized as an expert in his field. He is also recognized as a devoted Christian whose witness for Jesus Christ is clear and effective.

David Fisher is Director of RADAS and serves as editor-in-chief of script preparation. Because of his training and natural gifts, he is an ideal person to coordinate the exciting material obtained from a variety of Christian specialists.

There have been many books written on "science and the Bible," but this one is unique: it not only seeks to *defend* the faith, but also to *extend* the faith! The contributors are not simply experts in science, they are also "missionaries" of the gospel who are using their technical knowledge to pry open the minds and hearts of lost sinners so that the truth of God's Word might enter in.

As you read this book, you will learn a great deal about God and His marvelous creation. But I trust you will also learn to care about the spiritual needs of millions of people behind the Iron and Bamboo Curtains of the world. These radio programs were prepared not simply to educate, but to evangelize, to reach lost people *who perhaps could be reached in no other way.*

As you read, pray. Pray that God will use the ministry of RADAS to touch the lives of listeners and lead them to faith in Jesus Christ. Pray for believers in the communist world, many of whom are suffering for their faith.

"O send out thy light and thy truth!" (Psalm 43:3).

WARREN W. WIERSBE
Chairman of the Board,
Slavic Gospel Association

Associate Bible Teacher,
"Back to the Bible Broadcast"

Preface

This book contains the stories of men and women of science who have found life's fulfillment through faith in Jesus Christ, the Son of God.

The nature of the relationship between science and the Christian faith has become a major issue in our age. To some, the two pursuits are opposed and contradictory. But to many, they are harmonious and complementary.

Countless volumes have been written on the theological and philosophical aspects of the relationship between faith and science. Unfortunately, the levels of argument such works propound are often too abstruse or intellectual to meet the needs of more than a few who read them. Fewer volumes have addressed the interrelation between science and the Christian faith in a relatively simple and direct manner, through the *personal experiences* of people who are both scientists and committed Christians.

This book is of the second kind. It addresses the everyday practicalities of life and its possibilities, with testimonies from a range of scientists of lively and active Christian persuasion. Drawn from several different countries and continents, and from various areas of science, the testimonies focus on matters of great practical concern to the scientist and layman alike.

Each testimony was prepared first for use in RADAS, the Radio Academy of Science, a new evangelistic venture of the Slavic Gospel Association. Some of the authors are well-known international figures; others are engaged in quite commonplace activities; some are still students; and many will never make the world's headlines. But, clearly, each one of them is being blessed and used by God, even within his scientific discipline.

So this book is proffered to anyone, inside or outside the global church of Jesus Christ, who is seeking answers to key questions of the twentieth century. In order to share the message with as many people as possible around the world, the Slavic Gospel Association will apply all royalties to its missionary activities.

Since our goal is to continue to reach thinking people everywhere for Jesus Christ, we hope that this glimpse into the program scripts of the Radio Academy of Science will encourage many other Christian scientists to write to us, so that we can use their insights and experiences in our program also.

1

Flight to Faith

For *Dr. Boris P. Dotsenko,* an espionage exit from the Soviet Union was to prove an esoteric entrance into a personal relationship with God. Brought up under the ideology of scientific atheism, which he had "absorbed into the very marrow of his bones," Boris came to faith in the Creator and Sustainer of the universe through three surprise discoveries of the Bible—one in an old barn in the southern USSR, one in a professor's study in Leningrad, and one in a motel in Edmonton, Canada.

"Disillusionment with the ideology of materialistic Communism," says Dr. Dotsenko, "is that common factor in the lives of Soviet intellectuals who are finding God."

Dr. Boris P. Dotsenko *received his first academic degree in physics and mathematics at the University of Lvov, in the Soviet republic of the Ukraine, in 1949. He was awarded an M.Sc. degree at the University of Leningrad, and obtained his doctorate at Moscow State University in 1954 for research in physical and mathematical sciences.*

After working for three years in the prestigious Academy of Sciences of the USSR, on intercontinental and space rocket research, Dotsenko moved to the Institute of Physics in Kiev, where he was eventually appointed Head of the Nuclear Laboratory.

He sought political asylum in Canada in 1966, while he was traveling on official business. Since then, he has taught at a number of schools and colleges, including the Waterloo Lutheran University, in Waterloo, Ontario, and the University of Toronto.

Dotsenko is a member of a Mennonite Brethren Church.

During World War II, I lived in Siberia. Life was very hard. At the age of fifteen, I went to work on the construction of boilers for factory power plants. The moisture of the steam and the coal dust made it hard to see more than ten steps away. Food was scarce, and we were often very hungry.

I had always had a natural curiosity. In my harsh surroundings, I asked myself more than ever before, *Why do we live?* I read some of the works of Plato and Socrates, and I was thrilled with the clear, logical thinking of the Greek philosophers. But I was a convinced atheist; I had absorbed my political and antireligious thinking into the very marrow of my bones.

At the end of World War II, I was of university age. My family was "reevacuated" to the Ukraine. There I was able to enroll in an electrotechnical college.

One hot and humid afternoon in August, when I was at my grandfather's home recovering from a bout of pneumonia, I wandered into an old barn and fell asleep on a pile of hay. When I awoke, I discovered that I had slipped down between the hay and the rough wooden back wall of the barn. Struggling, I fell further to the floor. There, by my feet, I saw some old papers.

Reaching down, I found some copies of a very old magazine and parts of a book without a cover. Its pages, yellowed with time, were covered with two languages. One was strange, but I recognized it as Old Slavonic script. On opposite pages, in Russian, was a translation of the text. I read: "The gospel of Our Lord Jesus Christ..."

I was frightened. I knew that Christianity was frowned upon in my country. Churches had been burned down or closed. Christian preaching had become a crime, although I did not know why. But, at the same time, I was intrigued. I hid the book under my shirt and sneaked back to my room.

There I read more. The words of John 1:1— "In the beginning was the Word, and the Word was with God, and the Word was God"—struck right into my mind! Here was a very clear statement of what was at the beginning, underneath everything. But it completely contradicted everything that I had been taught! Psychologically speaking, reading that was an extremely shocking experience for me.

As I read on, I felt increasingly uncomfortable, and nearly ridiculous. It was so different from all I had been taught. I had thought that it was Stalin who had first said, "He who is not with us is against us." I discovered now that it had been Jesus Christ (see Matthew 12:30).

The Great Commandment of Jesus particularly frightened me. *How could I love God and my neighbor as myself if God did not exist?* I had been told that any enemy who does not surrender must be annihilated. I had learned that I had a responsibility to betray, if necessary, not only my neighbor, but even my own family. So I resisted what I read, but the words sank deep into me.

Then, strangely, after two weeks, the Scripture disappeared from my room. To this day I know neither how nor why it happened. But what I read had left its mark on me. I kept reverting to its implications while studying physics and mathematics at the University of Kiev.

One of the most fundamental laws of nature that interested me was the Law of Entropy, which is concerned with the probable behavior of the particles (molecules, atoms, electrons, and so on) of any physical system. Put simply, this law states that, left to itself, any physical system will decay with time; matter tends to become increasingly disorganized. (One of the implications of this law is that the whole material world should have turned into a cloud of chaotic dust a long, long time ago!)

As I thought about all of that, it suddenly dawned on me that there must be a very powerful *organizing* force counteracting this disorganizing tendency within nature, keeping the universe controlled and in order. This force must be nonmaterial; otherwise, it too would become disordered. I concluded that this power must be both omnipotent and omniscient: there must be a God—one God—controlling everything! I realized also that even the most brilliant scientists in the best equipped laboratories are still incapable of copying even the simplest living cell: God must be the Creator of life on Earth.

I did well in my studies at Kiev, and I received and accepted an opportunity to study further at the University of Leningrad.

While I was studying for my master's degree in Leningrad, I discovered another Bible in an unlikely place: the study of the late Dr. Jakov Frenkel, a Russian scientist of world reknown. I had been hesitant about deciding what priority God ought to have in the life of a scientist. It impressed me greatly that this brilliant man, who had the most intimate knowledge of the laws of nature, should keep the Book of God openly in his library.

I began to reach out to God through prayer.

In 1951, as one of the three best students at graduation in Leningrad, I was sent to Moscow State University. There I obtained my Ph.D. in physical and mathematical sciences in 1954, and was assigned to work in the Academy of Sciences of the Soviet Union. My field of research was intercontinental and space rocket research. My personal ideology continued to swing towards Christianity.

In the years that followed, I became a respected scientist, working in the nuclear branch of the Institute of Physics in Kiev. But I lost faith in others—and even myself—when I discovered that my father and my wife were reporting regularly to the KGB on my actions and beliefs.

By the fall of 1964, the strain had become intolerable. I prayed, "My God, kill me, or take me out of here!" I took an overdose of sleeping pills. When I regained consciousness in the hospital, I remembered saying also, "My Lord, Thy will be done."

Death had not worked. That in itself was an answer to my prayer. I decided to wait and see what God had in store for me.

In 1966, I was appointed Head of my laboratory—a great honor in itself. Then, one day, I was called to Moscow, to the Central Committee of the Soviet Communist Party. I was told that I was to be sent to Canada, and after that to Vienna, as a senior member of the International Atomic Energy Agency. From there, I would be expected to send back information about the achievements of nuclear researchers throughout the world.

One of the top men, Comrade Baskakov, lifting his finger to indicate a quotation from the highest source, said to me, "Boris Borisovich, we will be able to reward your service greatly—up to the Nobel Prize in Physics!"

Two days later, I was in Canada, at the University of Alberta. When I began to unpack my luggage in my Edmonton motel room, I found a third Bible—this one placed there by the Gideons, an international group of Christian businessmen who donate free Bibles to hotels and other public institutions in many countries of the world for the benefit of their clients.

My hands trembled as I lifted the Bible. It opened to John 1:1, and I was reminded of that verse which had struck me so forcibly twenty-two years before, in the Ukrainian barn: "In the beginning was the Word, and the Word was with God, and the Word was God." Thereafter, I spent every available moment absorbing the Word of God. Did I now accept what I read? I swallowed it all!

I became a Christian, and I was soon baptized by a minister in Edmonton, Alberta.

I quickly realized that my relationship with Jesus Christ was more important to me than my career, or even my beloved homeland and family. So I stayed in Canada and began teaching physics at several schools and universities.

Today I know that the Bible is the greatest Book of faith, in which the acts of God are recorded for believers. Its final proof will come with the return of our Lord and the establishment of His kingdom.

I believe that God is the Creator of the universe, but He is not *confined* to it. He is independent! He keeps and controls the whole universe, and each part that helps to make it up. He is the One who maintains its order. It is hard for us to conceptualize adequately His relationship with this world, because He does not belong to this "reality"—the only one with which we are familiar.

A simple analogy may help us to understand this a bit more clearly. Consider an electric field, with small particles of iron placed in it. The movements of the particles are controlled by that field, but the field itself does not become part of the system of particles. Each preserves its own "individuality." In the same way, man is circumscribed by God-ordained conditions, but he can still behave to some extent according to his own nature.

But no analogy can do justice to God's provision for men to enjoy spiritual union with Him. Paraphrasing Francis Bacon, one may say that superficial and egocentric knowledge leads to atheism, while genuine, deep, and objective study leads to faith in God. I thank Him for bringing to my attention three times, in different places and over many years, His book for the world, the Bible. And I thank Him too for granting me the faith to know Him personally and to experience His love. As a professor, I want to train my students in science. But, more importantly, I want to help them to become people who realize their chief responsibilities: to society, to the world around them, and—above all—to God Himself.

2

Cause and Effect

For many years, *Paul Adams-Jutzkiewicz* wandered the world, searching for real meaning in life. Pursuing that objective throughout many countries of the world, he became a rolling stone of sorts. Not surprisingly, he can say, "I like to think of myself as an expert hitchhiker: I've tried virtually every means throughout the United States and Europe." Eventually, "something unheard of in hitchhiking happened"—in answer to his first real prayer.

Before that happened, he gained a wider and more varied experience of life in six short years than most of us manage in a lifetime. Following his initial university studies in Newcastle-upon-Tyne and in London, Paul worked on twelve assorted jobs in six different countries. He found time to complete an M.Sc. degree in environmental resources—plus courses in biology, Red Cross first aid, and Spanish.

Paul says that, when he finally found the

truth about life, it came as a "dazzling revelation" to him. This is how he puts it: "A scientist's training equipped me to reach absolute truth concerning my own life—indeed, concerning life itself."

Paul Adams-Jutzkiewicz *was born in Derby, England, in 1951. His mother is English, but his father is Polish, having come to Britain from Warsaw in 1940 with the Free Polish Air Force.*

Paul graduated with an Honors Degree in Psychology from the University of Newcastle-upon-Tyne in 1973, specializing in animal behavior. He received a Postgraduate Certificate of Education from the University of London in 1974. From 1976 to 1977 he studied the behavior of urban foxes in Bristol and undertook an ecological survey of fresh water bodies for the Wigan County Council, while working towards his M.Sc. degree in environmental resources at the University of Salford.

His other activities between 1974 and 1980 make for amazing reading. He worked as a veterinary assistant and trainer for the Jacksonville Zoo in Florida. He helped to rehabilitate oiled sea-birds in Brittany, and he worked as a laboratory assistant in Marine Sciences in the University of Brest, France. He assisted on an oceanological research vessel, operating along the coast of Morocco, and he taught guitar at a public school in Switzerland.

Two years in succession, he won a Burroughs Prize for individual studies in natural history. A gifted linguist, he speaks eight different languages. Musically talented, he plays four different instruments. Physically active, he's good at athletics, swimming, and the martial arts.

He is now a science teacher at St. Vincent School in Gosport, England.

I am a teacher of secondary school science. The areas I cover are extensive—not that I'm an expert over such a vast range of study. No, I still have to do what I've always enjoyed doing. I have to continually seek out and learn more up-to-date facts; then I have to assess and teach them. Above all, I have to be *critical*. But I enjoy it, and my diverse experience is certainly an advantage.

The beginnings of my science career were shaped by my insatiable interest in natural history. By the age of twelve, I was already asking questions that my biology teachers could not answer. I progressed in my own research at home. My artistic ability and my love for languages, however, did present me with a dilemma in later years: *Which direction would I take for university?* Eventually, I chose what I thought was, for me, the easier option: science. But I continued to enjoy artistic pursuits—the guitar, drama, painting, and languages—in my own time. I often reckoned myself to be a scientist by circumstance, because I might have been just as happy with an arts degree.

My entrance to university was determined by my examination results in biology, chemistry, and physics. To tell the truth, I only just made it! At the age of eighteen, I found that the pull of fast living had almost become too much for me; girls, parties, and youthful fun had become priorities over my studies.

The odd thing was this: The prayer I had always repeated, parrot-fashion, night after night, since I was ten years old, still featured as my nocturnal obligation. I always prayed for high academic achievement, and I had never, ever, failed an examination since that time. However, my childhood belief in God had hardly survived—little more than a religious superstition remained.

In October 1969, I began my courses at the University of Newcastle-on-Tyne in the north of England. Zoology, physiology, and psychology were exciting studies at the university. I even managed to find a balance between those and all the other "delights" that the campus offered. Parties, dancing, and girls still featured high on my list. But, after four years of rather egocentric living—including a lot of travel to Europe and the United States—I like to think of myself as an expert hitchhiker!—I managed to gain an Honors Degree in psychology.

I went on to obtain a postgraduate teaching certificate at London University, and, after one year of teaching science, I undertook a Master of Science degree in ecology at the University of Salford.

Science is governed by well-defined rules. One is the premise that the basic principles we discover will always be true. We depend greatly upon the repeatability of experiments. We make predictions and thus discover the fixed laws of science. Science is based on *cause and effect*. All of my school lessons are based on that premise.

In physics, every pupil knows Newton's first law of motion: An object will remain in its state of rest or uniform motion until acted upon by a force. How beautifully that illustrates our principle of cause and effect: if you do not push your trolley, it will not move!

In chemistry, the principle is exemplified again. I have yet to see a precipitate forming in a silver nitrate solution without the presence of a causal agent like the chloride ion.

Our physics experiments show how the heating effect in an electrical conductor is caused by the excitation of subatomic particles. Along with heat, light energy is emitted—cause and effect again.

Thus, our scientific experiments display such orderliness that our very livelihoods can depend on it. We can and do expect very certain results to occur, time and time again. And we are not disappointed. Yes, variations may occur, if we change the conditions of any cause-and-effect relationship, but the patterns and predictions that we discover remain ever constant. The more I pondered this truth, the more I questioned its application to all areas of life—*my* life.

Where did this intelligent orderliness originate? Could order be part of my life? Were all of the events in my life governed by cause and effect? I wondered if religion could provide the answer. At that time, religion was a taboo subject for me.

To me, God was a name—nothing more. My

academic pursuits had reached an all-time low. I was out of work, pursuing very selfish and unworthy goals. The results were short-lived pleasures, long-lasting hangovers, broken relationships, selfishness, and, ultimately, utter loneliness.

I hitchhiked through Europe and Scandinavia on my downward path. There was no trace of optimism in my thoughts. In desperation, I began to question my personal convictions and the life I had been living. I knew I needed help. I began to wonder if God was real—and, if He was, if He would help me to do something better with my life. I was forced to admit that I had become very unscientific—*I had denied something that I had not put to the test!* I had rejected the possibility of God without ever examining the evidence.

Then a thought occurred to me. A year earlier, I had heard of a community of thinking people in Switzerland who claimed to have found a satisfying faith in God. I felt somehow drawn to that area near Lausanne.

But I didn't even know the address. All I knew was the name of the group, *L'Abri*—the French word for "The Shelter," referring to the large house owned by Professor Francis Schaeffer. There intellectuals who were sincerely seeking truth could search for it, under the guidance of this well-known Christian philosopher.

I sat by the roadside in the pouring rain—lost, and at the end of myself. I decided to pray and put God to the test. "If You're there, God," I challenged Him, "then You'll have to get me to L'Abri. I give up."

Within three minutes my prayer was answered. Something unheard of in hitchhiking happened: a *young lady* screeched her car to a halt and called out, "Do you need a ride somewhere?"

I was astonished, but I quickly recovered and told her where I wanted to go. She went out of her way to take me there—*up* the mountain, instead of down—and dropped me at the entrance of L'Abri Chalet. My experiment with God had proved successful!

At L'Abri I found a community of intelligent, thinking people, whose attractive lives were clearly the results of a cause-and-effect relationship. But what was the cause?

It was nothing I could rationalize through science—it was *God*. These people were happy. The successfulness of their way of life was undeniable. At first, I refused to believe that God could be the source of their success.

But the day came when I had to confess just how *unscientific* I had been: I had denied something that I had not tested properly. A basic rule in science has to be, "If you haven't tested something, then you can't knock it!"

Remembering the answer to my prayer on the road to L'Abri, I decided to pray again. Again I got an answer to my simple prayer. I prayed some more, and slowly my own daily life responded to some cause that I could not understand. The Bible gave me answers to life's problems. Doing things my own way had caused all of the negative effects from which I was running.

So, gradually I laid out all of my problems before this God I had not known, and one by one each answer came. I prayed to go back to England, and I received a phone call from someone with whom I had broken relationship *asking* me to return. I had no money, but within two weeks I was given teaching jobs and financial gifts from strangers. I prayed for understanding, and after two days at home I was making arrangements for my marriage. I prayed for my friends, and in one week a friend's business took a miraculous turn for the better.

So I became a believer in a God who responds to prayer, cares, and provides. I don't always understand His reasons, but my life is now enjoyable. It has purpose and direction. I've found fulfillment through *applying God's cause and effect*. He has ordered all things, and I would be foolish—not to mention unscientific—if I did not include Him in my life.

3

Seeing Things Differently

"Most people tend to look at things superficially, and they seldom take the trouble to look beneath the surface."

Such is the opinion of *Dr. Robert Selvendran,* a Sri Lankan researcher in plant biochemistry. For several years he has been concerned with the translocation of active metabolites (water and nutrients) from the roots to the aerial parts of tea plants and, more recently, on the composition of cell walls from organs of edible plants. He tells us that his work has heightened his interest not only in the aerial parts of plants—which we can see readily—but also in the underground organs, which we normally do not see, but which are essential, integral parts of each plant as a whole.

Robert explains how, when challenged to think deeply about two different religions, he came to appreciate God for the very first time. It was then that he saw the world, and his own life, in an entirely new and more complete way.

Today, he likens the research scientist who is a committed Christian to an evergreen tree. Rooted in Christ, his invisible "inner life" is sustained, even in adverse circumstances, by fellowship with God. And his "outer life"— that which is seen by his colleagues, family, and friends—exhibits a form and vigor determined by his spiritual union with God.

Dr. Robert Selvendran was born in the town of Jaffna, Sri Lanka, and received his primary and secondary education at Jaffna College, in Vaddukoddai. After obtaining a B.Sc. Honors degree in chemistry, with pure mathematics as his subsidiary subject, from the University of Sri Lanka at Colombo, he joined the Tea Research Institute of Sri Lanka at Talawakelle as a research assistant in biochemistry. He was offered a scholarship to undertake research at the University of Cambridge, England, and was awarded his Ph.D. in 1968. His thesis dealt with the "Metabolism of Phosphorylated Compounds in Strawberry Leaves." For his successful research, he was awarded the Broodbank Fellowship of Cambridge University for 1967 and 1968.

Today he works as Principal Scientific Officer at the Food Research Institute at

*Norwich, England, and has become a leading
international authority on plant biochemistry,
specializing in the chemistry of cell walls
in food plants. He has published over forty
research papers in scientific journals, including*
Phytochemistry; *the* Biochemical Journal;
Carbohydrate Research; Annals of Botany,
Chemistry, and Industry; *and the* Journal
of the Science of Food and Agriculture.
*He has also contributed review articles to
scientific textbooks. He has participated in
international symposia on carbohydrates and
dietary fiber in several countries of Europe,
Australia, and New Zealand, and has given
lectures on plant cell walls and dietary fiber in
several universities in the United States.*

*Nevertheless, one of Dr. Selvendran's
greatest interests lies in the relationship between
science and Christianity. He contends that
science is essentially a religious activity, which
plays its own special role in unfolding the
nature and purpose of God.*

I am a Sri Lankan; I took very little interest in Christianity and the Person of Christ, up to the age of eighteen years, despite the fact that I was born into a family that had a nominally Christian background. From the age of eight years or so, I knew that Christianity was real to my mother, but it seemed to mean very little to my father, and still less to my sister and brothers.

I was the youngest in the family and grew up to be indifferent to Christianity. In fact, I resented going to church services, because they did not mean anything to me at all; they always seemed dull and boring. The only evenings on which I found myself within the church were those when the church group prepared to go carol singing at Christmastime. It seemed like good fun to go carol singing. We were given plenty of snacks by the people we visited! But, apart from this annual event, Christianity seemed to hold very little promise for me.

Perhaps that was partly due to the fact that I lived in a village that had a predominantly Hindu population, and—so far as I could see—the lives of the Christians did not seem very different from those of the Hindus. Therefore, I thought that a person's religion was unimportant—and very much conditioned by where and when he was born. And none of us has any control over things like that!

I always avoided morning prayers at school, because they seemed empty and meaningless. In comparison, I found sports and outdoor life extremely engaging. I spent all of my spare time playing games, hunting birds, or picking berries and fruits—mostly from other people's gardens!

I became seriously interested in my schoolwork when I was about fourteen years old. The study of the various sciences really gripped me. I became especially interested in chemistry, physics, and pure and applied mathematics. Within a year, I was getting very high grades in those subjects and winning first prizes in them all. From that time on, the pursuit of scientific knowledge was uppermost in my mind.

I fared extremely well at the university entrance examination and gained direct admission to the University of Sri Lanka. In my first year at the University, I excelled in the sciences, won a scholarship, and qualified to do an honors degree in chemistry. I was really excited, because I had proved myself at the university level. The sciences seemed to hold a lot of promise to aspiring bright students, and I was determined to get to the top.

By contrast, religion in general, and Christianity in particular, meant almost nothing to me.

But this indifference to Christianity was to change completely when I returned home for one of the Christmas vacations. One of my close Hindu friends began talking to me about the virtues of Hinduism. He challenged the whole basis of my very nominal Christian faith. In fact, he clearly implied that my great-grandparents had been wrong in two respects: they had wrongly renounced their *Hindu* faith, and they had wrongly embraced a foreign religion, just because the missionaries and missionary schools offered "fringe benefits." He spoke very disparagingly of Christians, the church, and church activities. My friend felt that I ought to renounce my Christian faith and become a Hindu.

I must say that, as far as I was concerned, my Hindu friend seemed absolutely right. But for the first time in my life, I started thinking seriously about religion, and especially about Christianity. I concluded that I had to go to the "grass-roots" of Christianity. I had to think it through carefully, weigh the evidence, and then arrive at a decision that would seem most logical.

I told my friend of my intentions, and he seemed well pleased. He had no doubts about the outcome!

I began to read the Bible, primarily the gospels. I sought help from a teacher I thought was a committed Christian. He explained to me the implications of the birth, life, death, and resurrection of Jesus Christ—the One whom Christians believe was God in human form. He explained the activity of the Holy Spirit in the lives of Christians. He told me that Christ loved the whole world and gave His own life to redeem it, as the Bible states. He drew my attention to John 3:16: "God so loved the world that He gave His only begotten Son, that whoever believes in Him should not perish, but have eternal life."

Those views about Christ and God and the relevance of the death and resurrection of Christ were all new to me. The teacher proceeded to tell me that Jesus Christ loved me and died for my sins, so that I could become a true child of God and enjoy fellowship with Him forever. He particularly encouraged me to read the New Testament.

As I did so, I sought help from God. It seemed logical to suppose that if the Bible *was* God's Book, then surely *He* would help me to understand it better. And He did! As I continued to read, the historical Jesus started to become real to me. I distinctly remember the day I knelt down and prayed for God to show His love to me, to forgive my sins for Christ's sake, and to make me His child.

Soon after I said that prayer (and I really meant it), I became very conscious of the love of God, and the "scales," as it were, dropped from my eyes.

The joy that flooded my heart at that moment was absolutely tremendous. I had not experienced anything like that before. I knew for certain that God loved me in Christ and had made me a child of His affection. From that moment on, reading the Bible became a real pleasure for me—I literally couldn't put it down.

Reflecting on that phase of my life, I think that it is not unlike the thrill of making scientific discoveries. The first major discovery I made was with tea plants. And the tea plant seemed altogether different to me after I had come to appreciate some of its hidden secrets. In the same manner, the Bible now seemed to pulsate with new truth and life. Its central figure, Jesus, seemed to breathe new life into me. I couldn't help telling everyone what Jesus had done and was doing for me. Nothing else in the world seemed to matter except serving Him. In everything I did or said, He had to be first.

You may be wondering about my Hindu friend. I remember going back to him and telling him about my discovery—that I had found the truth about God, myself, and the world in the Bible. I had become a Christian because of what Christ had done for me, and He had effected a change in my life.

Of course, my friend dismissed all of that as a figment of my imagination, as most skeptics are inclined to do. But I knew that my experience was real. Christ had come into my life. He had changed my outlook on everything. Despite the person I had been, I now had a genuine love for others. I had begun to wish everyone well and to long sincerely that others too might enter this loving relationship with God and His people. To this day, nearly twenty-five years after I first asked Christ to come into my life, I haven't found anything *remotely comparable* to the joy of knowing God through Christ Jesus, my Lord and Savior.

After that revolutionary change in my view of life had taken place, I went on to complete my honors degree in chemistry. Later, I went to Cambridge University in England to obtain a Ph.D. in plant biochemistry. After my Ph.D., I did research for several years on tea. For the past ten years, my research has focused mainly on the chemistry of cell walls in edible plants, based at the Food Research Institute in Norwich, England.

I find research interesting, demanding, stimulating, and very exciting. My research work has taken me to various countries for participation in scientific meetings, and I have profited from visits to other laboratories.

I can claim that I have made several discoveries in my field, but none of them compares with *the greatest discovery I have ever made*. That happened in December 1958, when I discovered that Christ was indeed my Savior, Lord, and God—and not only *my* Savior, but the Savior of the whole world.

4

Forsaking Fallacies

Christianity is beset by three common fallacies.

The first maintains that adherence to the Christian faith usually depends on accidents of birth. If born in a "Christian country," it's likely—perhaps even inevitable—that an individual will become a Christian.

The second says that the Christian faith strains the credulity of modern man and that those most likely to become Christians are simple people who have led sheltered lives.

The third common fallacy contends that many people embrace Christianity for personal convenience or material gain.

Talib Barwani, from Zanzibar, Tanzania, in East Africa, is a living contradiction of all three fallacies.

Born in one non-Christian country, he became a Christian believer in another.

An intelligent, quick-witted man, he has worked in several technically-demanding areas of applied science, including military telecommunications and, more recently, electronical engineering. Living anything but a sheltered life, he had traveled completely around the world before he was twenty years of age.

And becoming a Christian was, for Talib, the *very opposite* of personal convenience. On returning home to share news of his newfound faith with relatives and friends, he had real cause to fear that someone would try to avenge the "shame" that he had inflicted thus on his family. He feared that his own people would try to murder him!

Talib Barwani is a native of Zanzibar, Tanzania. Trained in the British Royal Air Force in ground telecommunications, he worked subsequently in the fault-finding laboratory of Marconi, the international electronics company.

Called to Christian missionary work, Talib worked for six years as a studio technician in the south of France.

Today he serves his missionary society as an extension (deputation) secretary from his home in Loughborough, England.

I was born to a Moslem family in Zanzibar.

As children, we were taught how to pray to God, fast, and do good works. We were taught at the same time that the Scriptures the Christians have today are unreliable—that they have been changed and are not the original books ascribed to the prophets of old.

As I grew up, I began to wonder what the rest of the world was like. When I was still in my teens, I left home and traveled to India. Then I was fortunate enough to be able to work my passage on a cargo boat, in which I went around the world. I went back home and told everyone there of the wonderful marvels I had seen—including some wonderful marvels I had *not* seen! That was a great time for me. I was a hero for a while—until all of my friends had heard my stories a few times over. Then I had to go away again to gather more.

The next time I went again to India, and then back to Arabia. I worked for a while in the oilfields of the Persian Gulf. Then I decided to go on to Britain, in the hope that I might be able to study more and extend my academic education.

When I ran into problems with that plan, I joined the British Royal Air Force. I had already developed an interest in electronics, and after RAF training in ground communications, I was posted overseas—on my own continent, Africa! I was based at a station near Tobruk, Libya. While living in tents, the members of my company all became pretty close companions.

One night, when I returned to my tent, I saw one of my English friends there—one with whom I used to swim and go out. I was surprised to see him kneeling by his bedside, *praying!*

I waited for him to get up, and then I began asking him questions. *How had he suddenly become religious?* I wondered. I had not seen him praying before.

"I've not suddenly become religious," he replied. "I am a Christian!"

"Yes, but aren't you all? You were born in a Christian country!" I said. Because I had been born a Moslem, in a Moslem country, I thought that all of the people in Europe and America and other places were Christians by birth.

"No," he replied. "There's a real difference in our country between those people who are really Christians and those who are not. Many people who live in so-called Christian countries have no faith in God at all!"

I began to tell him about my creed and about our prophet and the book we considered authoritative. In return, he told me about the Christian faith. As far as I was concerned, we were simply exchanging notes on our respective religions.

But when he told me more about Jesus Christ, telling me that He was the only Savior, I became very angry. I had never heard anything so narrow-minded in my life!

Who do these Christians think they are, anyway? I thought. *Why should they think that they are God's favorites?*

I was making the common mistake of thinking that Jesus Christ was only for people who had been born in countries where a majority of the population is Christian. At that time, I did not realize that Jesus Christ really is the only true God—and the Savior for the whole world.

Then I came across another Christian airman. He had an open Bible in front of him. He explained to me that the Old Testament prophets spoke about Jesus Christ, and the New Testament part of the Christian Bible shows how those prophecies were fulfilled.

I didn't want to listen; I only did so out of politeness. But then the man came to a verse in the book of the Revelation of John. There Jesus says, "Behold, I stand at the door and knock; if *anyone* hears My voice and opens the door, I will come in to him and will dine with him and he with Me" (Revelation 3:20, italics added).

In spite of all of my preconditioning not to believe anything Christians might say, that verse went straight through all of my defenses. I had never realized that the Word of God had such power! I just knew that Jesus was the only Savior, and I needed His salvation.

But I could not admit a thing like that! This Christian I was talking to was dangerous: he had got me all agitated. I wanted to get away from him at once. I told him how nice it was to meet

him and thanked him for his time—all the sorts
of things one says, but does not really mean,
when one is saying good-bye.

So I escaped from him—but not from God! I
began to realize that my people say the Bible is
wrong because their holy book says different
things; they could not both be right. But the
Bible today is almost exactly the same as it was
two hundred years before my parents' faith was
founded, as ancient copies in the British Mu-
seum confirm. It could scarcely be a fault of
Christianity that it did not square with the holy
book of the Muslim faith.

The last book of the Bible contains dire warnings for any who might wish to alter the Christian
Scriptures. Because of those warnings, Christians would surely not dare to tamper with the
Book they said was the Word of God. I became
increasingly convinced that my people, too, are
those for whom Christ died.

Try as I might, I could not shake that verse
from Revelation from my mind. I went away one
day into a little Nissen hut that some Christians
were using as a church in the desert. Inside the
hut, I broke down and asked God to accept me
as one of His children, to forgive me for Christ's
sake, and to come into my life. At once I was
filled with tremendous joy and peace—something I had not experienced since I was a small
child.

But life was by no means all plain sailing from
then on. Most significantly, I wanted to go back
home and share my news with my family: I had
not been there for about four years. Back in Zan-

zibar I faced a time of difficulty and misunder-
standing. I was not in danger at home, because
we are a close-knit family and love each other.
But there was danger from those on the periph-
ery of the family. I was *really afraid* that someone
might take it upon himself to kill me. You see,
by leaving the faith of my family, I had become
an infidel, an *un*believer, and an outcast. I was,
therefore, a shame to my family, and it is permitted for such shame to be wiped out—literally
put to death! But the Lord protected me, and I
knew I could trust Jesus with my life.

I went over to the mainland of Tanzania, seeking Christians who would baptize me, and then
I returned to my base in Libya. As we live with
the Lord, He transforms all of our attitudes and
ways of thinking. I found that my outlook on life
had become completely different. I completed
my term in the RAF and went back to England
to further my work in electronics.

In the years that have followed, I have been
so encouraged as I have seen the Lord at work
in many different countries, in many different
ways. I believe this is God's time for the people
of my former faith everywhere. Just recently I
visited several churches in another country of
North Africa. It was great to share in fellowship
with believers there, to ask things, to learn
things, and to see the church growing and developing. Many of the leaders are young, but
they are spiritually mature and have clear spiritual vision. It's good to see that. The Lord is
building His church even in hostile environ-
ments.

There are many God-fearing people of other religions who are *just waiting* to receive the truth of the gospel. When my people realize that Jesus Christ is the Lord of glory, you *can't keep them away from Him!*

5

From Witches to Worship

Every science major is required to perform experiments. But *Ron Smith* experimented with things that his teachers never assigned. By comparison, the lethal laser he was building at the time of our interview seemed tame.

Sports have also played a major part in Ron's life. He holds his school's record for the hundred-yard dash, and he has national standing in the National Christian College Athletic Association (NCCAA).

RADAS Director Dave Fisher interviewed Ron Smith in October 1981, during Ron's senior year at Grace College, in Winona Lake, Indiana.

Ronald E. Smith *was born into a naval family. His own career is strongly inclined towards that branch of the United States armed forces.*

After graduating from United High School, in Armagh, Pennsylvania, Ron attended Grace College, in Winona Lake, Indiana. In 1982, he received his B.S., with a major in mathematics and a minor in physics. Following college, he studied at several specialized facilities of the US Navy: Officer Candidate School, in Newport, Rhode Island, from June through September 1982; Nuclear Power School, in Orlando, Florida, from October 1982 through April 1983; Naval Prototype Training Unit, in Idaho Falls, Idaho, from May through November 1983; and, most recently, Submarine School, in Groton, Connecticut, through November 1984.

On April 30th, 1982, Ron Smith married Julie Ann Lesh, of La Porte City, Iowa.

RADAS: Ron, how did you first become interested in science?

RON SMITH: I've been interested since childhood. My first-grade teacher recognized my interest and had me reading sixth-grade books in the first grade.

RADAS: What is your major here at Grace College?

SMITH: I'm majoring in mathematics and minoring in physics. I plan to go into nuclear engineering, so I've taken a lot of high-level math and done some work with mechanics and thermodynamics.

RADAS: Have there been any special projects that have really intrigued you?

SMITH: Yes. Right now I'm building a tunable-dye laser, and it's a real challenge. The concepts are easy to understand, but trying to get the pieces to match together is the hard part.

We will have to take many safety precautions with this laser. For example, we'll keep it behind double doors to prevent people from randomly walking into its path—because the beam will actually be powerful enough to cut a person in half. Also, the equipment around it will use such high voltage that accidently touching it could be fatal to a person.

We expect to use this laser in a three-dimensional photographic technique known as holography. It looks as if I'll be able to have it assembled by the end of the semester.

RADAS: After graduation, what are your career plans?

SMITH: The Admiral of the Nuclear Navy has offered me a job running the reactors on nuclear submarines. I feel quite honored about that, because there were more than a thousand applicants, and only twenty-nine of us were accepted.

That career goal will require another year of school after I graduate from college. Nuclear Power School is a really tough, twenty-four week program, and a person passes or fails on the basis of one final examination—four hours long.

RADAS: You seem like a person who enjoys competition.

SMITH: In high school I was really competitive. I loved to excel so much that whenever anyone would do better than I did on a test, I would become intensely jealous. Whenever people would ask me for help, I would refuse to help them, so that they wouldn't be so likely to beat me in a future exam. I even remember telling people *wrong* answers for tests!

When I was fifteen years old, I was really into the occult—things like astrological charts and horoscopes. I read a lot of books about witchcraft and casting spells—plus books on love, marriage, sex, and related subjects from an astrological perspective. I was involved in demon possession and learning to control demons by using magic symbols.

Many times, though, the situation would reverse itself, and the spirits would control me instead. At times, I really had no idea what I was doing. Passion controlled me, and I would say things and have no idea where I had picked them up. I had lost control of my words and actions to some power outside myself.

RADAS: When demonic influences controlled you, what kinds of things did you do?

SMITH: I feverishly pursued self-gratification—at any cost. I did things I'm ashamed of with several girls—not realizing that their bodies and mine were God's temples, and that God had commanded us not to defile them.

I was also very sarcastic and continually backbiting—saying malicious things that didn't help anybody and that really ate at me from the inside. I was filled with bitterness and self-centeredness.

Demons also made it easier for me to curse and use profane language. I hadn't heard a lot of profanity, but words I had never learned just seemed to flow naturally off my tongue. I memorized dozens of dirty jokes and repeated them over and over again. I still don't know what attracted me to that kind of material. It just seemed like a *compulsion*—an irrational urge overriding my will and my better judgment, and making me do things I later regretted.

Some of the people who used to participate with me have since been put into prison for murder. I could have gone the same way, if I had continued with them.

RADAS: How were you able to change?

SMITH: One day a high school friend invited me to a weeknight youth group meeting at his church. I went and was surprised that I actually enjoyed it.

When the pastor invited me to attend the Sunday services, I jokingly offered to come if he would visit my coven the night before. But I changed my mind and decided to attend church out of curiosity, without making the pastor attend my witchcraft meeting.

The church young people were participating in a series of Bible quiz competitions. I was surprised to discover that the Bible held a fascination for me, and I began reading and studying it.

The passages that fascinated me the most were those that dealt with demons and Satan. The Scripture seemed to cast Satan in quite a different light from that which I had seen him in before.

I had believed that God and Satan were

equals—always battling it out. Sometimes God won; sometimes Satan did; sometimes neither. But I discovered that the Bible paints a very different picture.

Satan is completely subject to God and does things only by God's authority. For example, in Job 1:12 and 2:6, God specified certain limits that Satan could not exceed in tormenting Job. I believe the incidents in Scripture that deal with demons are some of the best proofs for the deity of Jesus—proofs demonstrated in confrontation with His greatest foes.

The book of Revelation also fascinated me because of its supernatural images, accounts of miracles, and continual reassurance that God will win out over evil.

The first chapter of Genesis was probably the last of the passages that had a particular interest for me. As a science student, saturated with the theory of evolution, I looked at Genesis skeptically. But since God has enlightened my mind, I see the biblical account of creation as the story of God setting a perfectly-ordered universe into motion—with a complexity and precision that still defies total explanation by man.

When I read the passages about the crucifixion, I realized very movingly what Jesus had gone through as my substitute. I read the Bible's explanation of the crucifixion—"Greater love has no one than this, that one lay down his life for his friends" (John 15:13). That was the most convincing proof of love I had ever heard—that Someone loved me enough to give His life voluntarily for me!

On Christmas Eve in 1976, I publicly announced my decision to follow Jesus Christ.

RADAS: From being controlled by demons, to allowing Jesus to control you sounds like quite a change.

SMITH: A dramatic change! Some things happened immediately, and others took more time.

Right away, God started blotting evil things out of my mind. Over a period of time, God's Word began to influence my entire being. I wanted to discard the old things and just concentrate on the constructive things that God says in the Bible. I also *memorized* a lot of Scripture.

RADAS: What happened to all those filthy jokes?

SMITH: I don't remember any of them now. Even if I sit and think about them, I can't remember how they went or what the punch lines were. It's just amazing how God has wiped them out of my memory and replaced them with Scripture verses.

RADAS: The Bible speaks of "renewing your mind" and having it "transformed."

SMITH: Yes, and I think my case is a perfect example of that. God has been casting out the old things and putting new things in their place. The things I think about now help me through the difficulties of life. They're certainly a lot more helpful than an off-color joke ever was.

Academically speaking, God has renewed my mind as well. I failed math in second and third grades and got poor grades in it throughout grade school.

Then, all at once, in high school, God started working through me. I started getting "C's," then "B's," and all my college math has been "A's." I couldn't remember how to divide fractions in the second and third grades, but now calculus makes sense to me. God has renewed my mind intellectually, too.

I'm still a competitive person. During the last few years, I have set a new school record in the hundred-yard dash. I have gained national standing in the National Christian College Athletic Association (NCCAA). But when someone beats me in either an athletic event or a test, I no longer feel bitter resentment. Now I can congratulate the winner for having done a fine job.

RADAS: Is it ever a struggle to keep your mind under control?

SMITH: Yes, especially at times of the year like Halloween. A lot of people doubt the existence of demons and other evil spiritual beings. But I realize that I once played with fire, and that I can still get my fingers burned if I don't rely completely on God's power to protect and empower me.

I also see the ramifications in my attitudes— in rebellion against authority and things like that.

Last year when I was called to Washington D.C. for my technical interviews for nuclear engineering, I knew that the selection process was rigorous. From over a thousand applicants, they had selected only thirty-seven of us to go to Washington, and I felt a lot of anxiety over the thought of having all my scientific knowledge put to the test. Yet I constantly thought of the verse, "Be still, and know that I am God" (Psalm 46:10). That comforted me in the knowledge that God had control of my life, and that He would put me wherever He could use me the most effectively.

When the pressures of school seem to be too much for me, when my test grades aren't as good as they ought to be, when I can't comprehend new concepts, and when homework just keeps piling up—I simply claim Philippians 4:13: "I can do all things through Him who strengthens me." Jesus does strengthen me—body, soul, mind, and spirit—and He helps me to meet problems squarely with His strength.

6

The Axiomatic God

English college lecturer *Anne Sweeney* asserts
that our society is on the verge of a completely
new way of life. She sees evidence for this
in the classroom, where the pocket calculator is
revolutionizing what can and must be taught
in her subject, mathematics.

As a secondary school teacher, she greatly
enjoyed "Parents' Day" each year—when
mums, dads, and guardians came to discuss
the progress of her pupils. But she knew that
some of them would always complain that
their children were not learning the kinds of
things that they themselves were taught in
school. Many parents feel that the use of
calculators is somehow "cheating," and that
mathematics is not "proper mathematics"
anymore.

Anne points out that resistance to change is
nothing new. Jesus Christ once remarked
that people are like old leather wineskins; fill
them up with the wine of innovation, and they

crack up! "Fresh wine requires fresh skins" was His message.

Anne herself was renewed—outside as well as in—after realizing that God was not a *theorem* to be proved before He could be trusted—but an *axiom,* a truth, and a reality, whether He is trusted or not. She now understands how and why many who have trusted Him have been prepared even to die for their faith.

Anne Sweeney *is a native of Aberdeen, Scotland. She is now lecturing in mathematics at Chichester College of Technology in the south of England.*

After reading for a degree in mathematics and science at the University of Aberdeen, she received her Postgraduate Certificate and Diploma in Education from Aberdeen College of Education. She taught for one year in Scotland before moving south with her husband, David, who is also highly "numerate." He is head of computing at the Glasshouse Crops Research Institute, in Littlehampton, Sussex, England.

Together they are active members of the nearby Angmering Baptist Church.

From as far back as I can remember, I have always wanted to be a teacher. Mathematics has always held a peculiar *beauty* for me, a satisfying logic in all its facets. Unlike most girls, I always enjoyed taking things apart and seeing how they worked. Nothing has fascinated me more than learning how mathematical knowledge is built up into incredibly complex structures from relatively few simple axioms.

It is my nature to question things, to demand proofs, and to wrestle with conundrums. When I was only eleven years old and in my first year of secondary school, I encountered the first mathematical "mystery" to excite and amuse me. I was shown how to calculate the diagonal length across a square. Promptly, I drew a one-inch square and discovered that I could approximately *measure* the diagonal, but I could not *calculate* it: $\sqrt{2}$ is an "irrational" number, one that cannot be expressed exactly as either a fraction or a decimal figure. To my young mind, it seemed that I could draw a length that could not be represented by a number! I was puzzled, but intrigued.

Since then, I have learned many of the important "theorems" of mathematics. And I have learned many times that just because I cannot *prove* a theorem to my own satisfaction doesn't mean that it's false! Often I have been forced to turn to those more knowledgeable than myself for the answers and explanations. Regrettably, there are some things that I still fail to understand fully. Even so, that has not quelled my enthusiasm for my subject: I still enjoy the scent of the mysterious.

My father also taught mathematics for a time, and it was he who first taught me to love the subject. Meanwhile, my mother taught me to love God. However, as I grew up, I turned my questioning mind to examine all that I had learned about religion. I could prove for myself that many of my father's words about mathematics were true, but what about my mother's words about God?

If I really believed that what she said was true, then the logical conclusion—as I saw it—was that I should be prepared to *die* for my faith. I read in the Bible about martyrs. Some Christian believers were tortured for refusing to renounce their faith. Others suffered mocking, scourging, and even chains and imprisonment.

I asked myself, "If I were tortured, would I accept release by *denying God?*"

I knew that I would.

Therefore, I concluded there must be something fundamentally *different* between the faith of the martyrs and mine. If put to the same test, the outcomes of their faith and mine would be totally different. Long did I agonize over this. I was diligent in religious study and observances. I became fully acquainted with the doctrines of the church. I prayed regularly. But would I end it all for Jesus? Still the answer came from my heart—no, *never!*

An unexpected event jarred me to maturity. I had married while my husband was still a university student. I fully expected that when he graduated he would find work locally. I was filled with dismay when he accepted a job six hundred miles away, at the other end of Britain. On the TV weather maps, the south of England seemed like another world from the north of Scotland, where I had grown up. I would be so far from home. So that move meant I left behind all my previous Christian companionship and peer pressure to conform to the standards of the Bible. In my new loneliness I declared that I had been led falsely into believing there was a loving God in heaven. Either He didn't exist, or He was an *impersonal* spirit who didn't care about me!

But God is strong. He fights with us until we surrender to His superior strength. He does not depend on our thoughts for His own survival. Man cannot think God into existence—or imagine Him into nonexistence.

It is not natural for the materialistic mind to believe in Him, but to the inquiring mind God reveals His existence. When one man turned to Jesus and called Him divine, Jesus answered: "Flesh and blood did not reveal this to you, but My Father who is in heaven" (Matthew 16:17).

Slowly, it began to dawn on me that I was attempting the impossible. I was trying to prove the existence of God like a mathematical *theorem*, but He is more like an *axiom, a self-evident truth*

that needs no proof! In order to understand anything spiritual, we must first believe that God is
real.

I also began to realize that I deal daily with
abstractions and intangibles. For example, as a
mathematician, I have never "touched" the number 2. I have never seen it, and I find it incredibly
difficult to define without reference to other
numbers. Yet I believe in the properties of "two-
ness"; it is a vital part of the whole number system.

Why is it less logical to believe likewise in God,
invisible and intangible though He may be to
our physical senses?

Therefore I decided to believe that God exists,
and to try to contact Him through prayer. He
rewarded my searchings with *assurance* of His
presence. Such an assurance cannot be put into
words; it cannot be handled, smelled, tasted, or
heard. Rather, it is a bit of God Himself that He
gives us, mentally and spiritually, so that to deny
His existence becomes as unnatural for us as to
deny our own existence would be.

Thus I became convinced that God exists. By
definition, He must have existed before men
and indeed created us. It follows that if He created us, then He must *own* us. If He owns us,
He must *rule* us. So I offered God my alle-
giance—not at first because I loved Him, but
because I knew I had *no choice.* He ultimately was
my ruler—in my history studies I had heard of
the horrors awaiting trai-tors! I decided to serve
Him willingly.

I read again of the martyrs. *How could they do*

it? I wondered. *How could they experience God so vividly that His will was more important than their very lives? How could God be so important to them that they would choose to give up life rather than to give up their loyalty to Him?* I had begun to understand man's serving God on Earth, whether by constraint or not. But to die for Him? I could still neither accept nor understand that.

What finally changed my outlook was reading something Jesus said before His crucifixion. He prophesied that He would return, having made a new Earth, to bring this one to an end.

God's first creation had the capacity for good or evil, but His second creation will have the capacity for good only. Suddenly I realized that I could have no part in His second world, because I was intrinsically evil: I still put myself first.

I used to blame God for all the suffering in the world. Now I realize that it is those of us who live for ourselves that cause suffering, not God. Does God make my mother cry when I say cruel things to her in an argument? No, it is I who hurt her. Does God make the old lady down the road die of hypothermia? No, it is I. I could have bought her coal, but I didn't care enough.

Every action in my life seemed to turn and accuse me. I wondered if I would perish with the rest of the universe when Christ returned.

Again I thought of the martyrs. They were human like me, so they must have done evil like me. But clearly *they did not fear meeting God by death!* Why not?

For the first time I looked closely at the death

of Jesus Himself and concluded that there must
have been a purpose in it. If Jesus was God, tired
of a human frame, surely He could have just left
His body behind one day and become a spirit
again. Why did He endure a prolonged and
painful death?

As I thought about that I realized a wonderful
thing. Jesus, the pure, was punished for crimes
He did not commit; He died deliberately, willingly, to spare *us* from the just penalty of the
crimes that *we* have committed!

I had feared that when I saw God after death
He would play back a kind of audiovisual tape-
recording of my life, forcing me to watch it under
the scrutiny of His disapproval. I cringed at the
thought of some of the things I had done, and
I realized that they would condemn me to an
eternity of remorse. I begged for God's forgive-
ness because of the death of Jesus on my behalf.

When I looked at my life again, it was as if the
tape had been edited, and only the good bits were
left. I felt God's presence near me, rewarding
me for the good things in my life, but I called
out, "No, this isn't justice. I have done *wrong* as
well as right!"

But it was as if God made me look at the new
tape while saying, "I see no evil. *Jesus has cleared
the tape.*"

Why did those martyrs die? Like me, they had
concluded that it was foolish to deny God merely
because He could not be seen. But more than
that, they understood the love and mercy of God,
realizing that earthly suffering lasts only for a
relatively short time. They looked forward to the

everlasting home that Jesus was preparing for them, the home in which the Bible says, there "dwells no sorrow." Now I, too, can look forward to an eternity with Him—and if I had to die for Him, I would.

I have faith in the mathematics I teach, even though it is all based on *unprovable* axioms. But an axiom may be defined as "a *self-evident truth.*" Having accepted the axiom, the self-evident truth, of the reality of God's existence, I have obtained a far more important faith. I have faith in the living God, for whom I am now prepared to live—or even to die.

7

"I Couldn't Help Others Because I Couldn't Help Myself!"

Susan Steinmetz is a scientist who is very happy in her work. "Meteorology is a special thing in my relationship with the Lord," she says. "It's a product of my faith—and a means God uses to teach me more about Himself."

Her research is focused on water in the atmosphere. Even over the driest areas of the world there is water in the air. But it will only water the surface and bring life to it if it condenses and falls as rain. How does it condense? "Around tiny 'dust' particles which have an affinity for water," explains Sue. "The Bible speaks of man as 'dust'—and Jesus as 'living water.' When our affinity for Him is satisfied, we can help to refresh a spiritually barren world, too.

"I'm especially fascinated by the symbolism of the rainbow. Physically, the rainbow results from the prismatic effect of light from the sun. And, in the days of Noah, God first used it as a spiritual symbol—that He would never again threaten universal judgment by water because of sin. His enlightenment shines through believers: we are all witnesses to His grace and goodness. But it is sobering to remember that, in Noah's time, only a few people were saved. How were they saved? By doing what God said they should!"

Susan Steinmetz *is a research meteorologist in the Applications Laboratory of the United States National Oceanic & Atmospheric Administration (NOAA) in Washington, D.C. Her current research program is aimed at a better understanding of data from vertical profiling instruments on the NOAA series of meteorological satellites.*

She also participates in instructional programs, training the staffs of regional weather centers throughout the United States in new techniques for handling and analyzing data from weather satellites.

Miss Steinmetz gained her B.S. degree in meteorology, mathematics, and physics from Pennsylvania State University, and worked with NOAA under a cooperative studentship scheme before joining the staff at the World Weather Building on a permanent basis in 1979.

56

Sue shared her testimony with Dr. Eric Barrett, Dean of RADAS, during one of his professional visits to NOAA as a Contractor on a satellite applications project.

Her church is the New Covenant Christian Community in College Park, Maryland.

Imagine a top scientific laboratory in a government establishment—a veritable hot-bed of new ideas and approaches. Imagine especially an *open-plan* laboratory, laid out to encourage quick-fire exchanges of information and arguments—a place where *mental and physical restlessness* is actively encouraged. The Applications Laboratory of the National Environmental Satellite, Data, and Information Service of the US Department of Commerce, located on the outskirts of Washington, D.C., is just such a place.

But within that place we've found one peaceful corner. Let's meet its occupant, *Susan Steinmetz,* and ask her about the source of her calm demeanor. Why is it, too, that her co-workers, many of them her scientific seniors, often approach her for help with their personal problems?

RADAS: Susan, we understand that you are researching a space-age aspect of meteorology. Is that true?

STEINMETZ: Yes. I'm helping to interpret satellite images of water vapor in the atmosphere so that weather forecasts can be improved in areas where we get few observations from surface weather stations or balloons. Water vapor is normally invisible in the atmosphere, but there are infrared sensors on satellites today which can show where this gaseous form of water is concentrated. They do it by measuring the invisible heat radiation given up by the water molecules.

RADAS: That sounds very interesting. Was it always your ambition to become a research meteorologist?

STEINMETZ: No, it certainly wasn't. I was always keen to do something practical, to help people, and to do something meaningful with my life, but for many years I know I was failing miserably. In high school, my biggest achievement was a successful five-year campaign lobbying for a Coca-Cola machine! Even then I knew that there must be better things to do with my life. But I seemed incapable of helping people without hurting them. I had good intentions, but I broke promises, and many of my efforts ended in failure.

I got good grades at my studies, though, and studied for two years at Millersville State College, in Pennsylvania, before transferring to Pennsylvania State University to study for a Bachelor of Science. More important, though, I grew wise enough to call on God to help me make my life a success.

RADAS: You mean you made a conscious decision to become a Christian, and that made the vital difference?

STEINMETZ: That's right. I had been brought up in a loving and "moral" family, by "religious" parents. But that didn't mean I knew God myself. Indeed, I had little or no contact with true Christians. We "said grace" at meals, but didn't really pray. My parents didn't go to church—and I didn't see enough in people that I thought were Christians to want to go myself.

When I was fifteen or sixteen years old, I began to hear about people who lived really dynamic Christian lives, and I wanted to do so, too. But I didn't know any of those people, or how to get that power I knew I didn't have in myself. I began to read the Bible alone, because I figured that somehow it held the answers. But then I grew so busy with my school and college studies that I had no time to pursue my search for anything as nebulous and elusive as faith in God.

When I was at college, it really hit me that my efforts to help other people had failed. I had good intentions, but they often ended in hurts for others. I lacked the wisdom and strength to do what was best. I was suddenly overwhelmed with the realization that I couldn't help other people because I didn't even know what to do with my own life.

Eventually, I called out to God to direct my life, although I didn't know much about Him then. He was not so much a person as a *possibility*. But I was prepared to believe that He had made me and, therefore, that He loved me. *Surely He must understand me better than I do myself,* I thought. *He'll know how my life can become worthwhile!*

RADAS: Do you think it was God who directed you to your career in meteorology?

STEINMETZ: I'm *sure* it was! And the way He did it convinces me that He has a sense of humor, too. I was walking down a college corridor, past the meteorology department. Suddenly I found myself laughing. *Wouldn't it be funny if I became a meteorologist?* I thought.

I took one course in it, just to meet a general science requirement, and fell in love with the study of the atmosphere. It was perfect for me—awesome, scientifically challenging, and valuable to the community in a practical sense. I'm convinced that God led me to that decision.

RADAS: Then you were given the chance to transfer to one of the top schools of meteorology in the United States to continue your studies?

STEINMETZ: Yes, and it was while I was at Pennsylvania State University that I came to know God as I do now—as a really *personal* helper and friend. I became a new person under His direction and control. So it was through His instruction to study meteorology—and my obedience to it—that I became aware that He could help me in every aspect of my life. And it has been through meteorology that I have met the key people who have helped me to grow in my knowledge and understanding of Him. Now I am trying—and, I think, succeeding—to help others to find Him, too. I just wish that more people could know Him and love Him as I do.

RADAS: And so you have come to work on a practical problem in one of the most innovative centers of applied meteorological research in the world.

STEINMETZ: Yes, the Applications Laboratory is a really exciting place to be. In my group alone, there are four other scientists, all researching new uses of satellite data in areas like flash flood forecasting, coastal fog forecasting, and radiation and temperature monitoring for crop prediction. Other groups deal with other problems—monitoring ice and snow, forest fires, agricultural disease conditions, tornado hazards—the list is almost endless! We often discuss these areas in our seminars. I really thank God that He has given me peace of heart and mind, many opportunities for witnessing, and work that has real practical value.

RADAS: And we thank Him for the use He is making of you through your Christian witness and example in that hectic laboratory. We, too, are sure that it is God who gives all of us the answers that we need for life's most pressing problems. It is through Him that we can be most useful to others. What changes He can bring about! And these cannot be called rare, because a dramatic change can be expected in the life of any person who becomes an instrument of God.

The apostle Paul experienced a dramatic change in his life, too, when he committed himself to God's care and affection. He wrote this:

> And so, dear brothers, I plead with you to give
> your bodies to God. Let them be a living sacrifice,
> holy—the kind he can accept. When you think
> of what he has done for you, is this too much to
> ask? Don't copy the behavior and customs of this
> world, but be a new and different person with a
> fresh newness in all you do and think. Then you
> will learn from your own experience how his ways
> will really satisfy you. (Romans 12:1-2, *The Living
> Bible*)

8

Anxious for Nothing

Swimming lessons frightened him. Thunderstorms terrified him. His anxiety and pessimism kept him "playing it safe" and avoiding risks and new situations. His whole life was restricted by his fears.

Joseph Scott Greeson, a graduate student at Colorado State University, tells RADAS Director Dave Fisher how he overcame his crippling handicap of fear and anxiety.

Joseph Scott Greeson *graduated from Indiana University with a degree in physical geography, the science that deals with climate and other physical features of the earth.*

He has completed coursework toward his M.S. in atmospheric science at Colorado State University and is now completing his thesis on "The Vertical and Temporal Characteristics of Winter Orographic Clouds, as Assessed by Vertically-Pointing Radar."

RADAS: Joe, I understand that one of your major research projects involved studying snow in the Rocky Mountains. What was the goal of that research?

JOE GREESON: The Rocky Mountains represent the major water source for hundreds of thousands of square miles of land. We were looking at the feasibility of modifying the weather to increase the snow pack—the amount of snow that falls in those mountains—and especially to increase the water content of that snow.

We injected silver iodide (formula AgI) into clouds, attempting to convert the water in the clouds to ice. The goal was to produce precipitation at the times and places where it would be most useful.

RADAS: What kind of results did you have?

GREESON: Well, it's very difficult to tell yet. We're working with a highly-variable natural system. For example, one of my professors likes to say that, in a very wet year in the mountains, you get about *twice* the normal snow pack. In a very dry year, you get about *half* of the normal. So you're dealing with a variability of about 4 to 1.

It is hypothesized that we might be able to increase the snow pack in any given year by as much as 20 percent. So, to find the 20 percent man-made variation on top of a natural variation of about 400 percent is very difficult.

For example, if a particular year has 120 percent of normal precipitation, that could mean either of two things. Either nature did an average winter's work, and *you added 20 percent,* or the natural snow was above average for the year, and *you achieved nothing.*

So, to reach meaningful conclusions, the experiment will have to continue for several years, and we'll have to evaluate the long-term data very analytically.

RADAS: Scientists have a reputation for taking nothing for granted, but exploring every possible explanation for the events they observe. Do you ever carry that "show me" attitude into activities outside the laboratory?

GREESON: Yes. Sometimes we're accused of being argumentative.

I'll have to admit that the first time I attended an extracurriculur Bible study as an undergraduate at Indiana University, I went there to argue. I thought that the group members were being too closed-minded about the Bible as a source of truth and that they ought to be open to a lot of *other* sources of truth.

But, as I read through the Bible for myself, it became very clear to me that the Bible was written over an extremely long period of time. And yet it was *integrated*, rather than fragmented. As we were studying the book of Romans, our teacher pointed out that the principles in that book correlated with the principles of the Old Testament. I discovered things in the Old Testament that were models of what Jesus Christ later did—as recorded in the New Testament.

Seeing that unity—that totality—convinced me that there was a single mind behind the Bible. It was more than a collection of contributions from independent individuals at different geographic locations coming up with their own ideas in various centuries. Approximately forty different authors participated in writing the Bible, yet the remarkable wholeness and singularity of its message is inescapable.

RADAS: Does the Bible say anything about the science of meteorology?

GREESON: Yes, and that surprised me—considering the Bible's age, and yet the accuracy of that specific passage.

Without using modern words—like "evaporation," "condensation," and "precipitation"—one passage describes the results of those processes in these words: "All the rivers flow into the sea, yet the sea is not full. To the place where the rivers flow, there they flow again" (Ecclesiastes 1:7). My twentieth-century scientific mind recognized that the writer of that passage must have had quite an understanding of the interaction between water on earth and water in the sky.

From the very first Bible study, I also began to realize the relevance of the life, death, and resurrection of Jesus Christ for my life. His life was an active force—far beyond just being an example or a good role model to be followed. I realized at that very first study that Christ's life had an effect on the nature of my relationship with God and on the way that God saw me.

The fact that sin was still an active force working on my life—and that my sin needed to be dealt with so decisively that it took a crucifixion to overcome it—struck me very forcibly.

I had never realized those things before I read the book of Romans and saw how they applied to me personally.

RADAS: What was the pivotal point of your Bible study?

GREESON: I think it must have been when I decided to take those truths from the realm of the theoretical and move them into my personal life.

At first I was getting together with the people in the study to argue with them and to discuss some of the points—like another scientific abstraction—to be proved and disproved for my intellectual satisfaction. But then the Bible demonstrated over and over again to me that it was believable—that I needed to take it seriously. I saw the need to apply the Bible to my life—not just to believe in it as a scientific theory, but to depend on it, trust it, and allow it to become active in my life.

Several changes took place in my life. One was a new desire to find out more of what the Bible says. Naturally, my curiosity grew enormously because of some misconceptions that I had about what the Bible said. I was amazed when I discovered some things that it actually *did* say.

RADAS: For example?

GREESON: Well, I think my biggest misconception was that I had visualized the relationship between God and man as a set of rules—a list of do's and don'ts. If a person did everything—or most of the things—on the list, then he was all right with God. If he didn't do them—or didn't do enough of them—then God condemned him.

I can understand now that, according to the Bible, there is a reality of sin, and *every* person has to deal with it. It's not that some people have to deal with it, and others are good enough that they don't. Everybody has to face this question. Everyone has to deal with the sin in his life. Everyone needs to know how the relationship with God, which had been hindered by sin, can be restored.

When I was reading Jesus' Sermon on the Mount, in Matthew 5-7, I noticed His emphasis on guilt. He said that we are responsible for our thoughts, not just our actions. If a man hates his neighbor, he is guilty of sin—as guilty as if he had killed the man. And a lustful thought is as evil as an adulterous act.

RADAS: How did you react when you realized that you were guilty?

GREESON: My natural reaction would have been to despair in God's condemnation and give up all hope of a relationship with God.

However, I also realized that I needed to get rid of that guilt somehow. I understood that God really wanted to establish a relationship with me—a communicative relationship. In essence, I said, "Jesus, I understand that You died for me and for my sins. I want Your death on the cross to apply to my life. I know that that's the only thing that's going to eliminate this problem—this barrier of sin that stands between You and me. I want to apply that remedy to my life."

Now God can see me as a guiltless person, because Jesus Christ has transferred my guilt to Himself.

RADAS: What kind of changes have occurred in your life since you prayed that?

GREESON: I used to be a very anxious person. Whenever a thunderstorm came along, I would always be afraid that our house was going to be destroyed by a tornado. I used to worry about a lot of things. I was a very pessimistic person.

When I was eight years old, my parents enrolled me in a swimming class. I was so terrified of the water that I became convinced that I would eventually drown.

While the other children in the class were learning to swim well, I was too scared even to attempt it. I used to pretend that I was sick on the days swimming class met so I wouldn't have to attend. It didn't take much pretending to accomplish that, because my intense anxiety kept me on the edge of being physically ill.

But since Christ has come into my life—since I've been reading the Scripture and understanding God's power and complete control of every circumstance—I understand that He doesn't want us to worry about those things. As a result, I now have great freedom to try things that I wouldn't have done before. I have a real boldness in living, knowing that God is in control and cares about my situation.

RADAS: Were there any particular verses that He used to impress that on you?

GREESON: Yes. "Be anxious for nothing, but in everything by prayer and supplication with thanksgiving let your requests be made known to God" (Philippians 4:6). I have found an outlet for my anxiety, and I understand that God is in control. The universe isn't impersonal or random. There really is a God who cares about me individually—who's in charge of the things that go on around me.

RADAS: Isn't it conceited to believe that God could be concerned about you personally? After all, there are more than four billion people on

Earth. How could He possibly concentrate on you?

GREESON: If He were anything less than God, then certainly He would have to concentrate on some people by ignoring others. We humans can pay attention to only one person at a time.

But the God revealed in the Bible is *infinite*. He can concern Himself with even the minutest details of all of our lives—at the same time.

I was very much aware of His help in a field project I was doing, gathering weather data via radar. One time I had to operate three complex weather radars simultaneously. I was familiar with our university's radar, but I had to learn the operation of the two National Oceanographic and Atmospheric Administration (NOAA) radars in a matter of hours. It was an awesome responsibility, and one that I normally would have shied away from. But I claimed the scriptural promise, "I can do all things through Him who strengthens me" (Philippians 4:13). I learned the operation of those radars and the computer that went with them in the few hours available.

Before I came into living contact with the living God, I didn't have the kind of self-confidence that a situation like that radar assignment requires. And before I gave Christ control of my life, I certainly would never have had the courage to participate in an interview like this for publication and broadcast.

But that's just as well. Because before those things happened, I really had nothing *worth talking about!*

9

In Search of Truth

The search for truth has always been in the forefront of the thinking man's mind. He has looked for truth and has seen and used it in different shapes and forms. The French philosopher Montaigne once said that "Man is born to enquire after truth."

But truth is often seemingly relative. It recedes tantalizingly as we approach it.

Dr. David Tonge came to a point in his life when he felt discontented and curiously unfulfilled. As a scientist, he wondered if truth is something that really can be grasped. He asked himself what truth really is.

Eventually, by seeking, he came to realize that truth is not something that can be formulated or defined; it can only be *experienced* by those who accept it as a gift from God. Genuine truth enters a life when that life becomes "born again." Then truth is lived out in daily practice through a share in the almighty power that once transformed the dead man Jesus into the risen Lord of glory.

Dr. David Tonge *is a native of the principality of Wales. He studied as an undergraduate at Imperial College, London, obtaining a B.Sc. with First Class Honors in mathematics in 1956. After working as an applied mathematician in a British Admiralty Electronics Laboratory and with the Central Electricity Generating Board, he moved to the Department of Mathematics and Computer Science in the Polytechnic of Wales, near Cardiff. He has been employed there as a lecturer since 1965.*

It was at the Polytechnic that he first became interested in the problem of understanding the encoding and use of visual information supplied to the brain. Some of his theories have been published recently in the International Journal of Man-Machine Studies. *In 1979 he was awarded a Ph.D. degree by the University of London. He is now pursuing further his research interests in the fields of cognitive processes and artificial intelligence.*

Dr. Tonge is married and has two teenage daughters. He is a member of an evangelical church, where, since his conversion in 1976, he has been involved with youth group work. He is also active in Christian outreach through hospitals and among alcoholics.

What is the relationship between the *mind* and the *brain*? What are the differences between the two?

Scientists who work in a variety of fields—from psychology to cybernetics—have thought about that problem from time to time. We now know quite a lot about the *brain*. Although it is not a very imposing organ to look at, its complexity is formidable. Its secrets are chemical, electrical, and structural. Neurosurgery has revealed that the brain is composed of a network of electrically interconnected cells, or "neurons," embedded in a jelly-like substance. This visible and *tangible* structure is the location of that part of ourselves which is *intangible*—our conscious being: our thoughts, feelings, and will—all that we call *mind*. This is much more difficult to investigate, for the secrets of the mind are functional; they are locked up more securely in the way that the brain works.

My own first encounter with these intriguing problems occurred several years ago when I began to research problems of visual perception. My work was mathematical, concerned with constructing a theory about how visual information is stored in the brain. Within a few years, some of my results were published, and I had registered to submit a doctoral thesis to the University of London. This new research activity meant that my academic life as a lecturer at a Polytechnic became much more interesting. My life was fuller, and I was a busier, more fulfilled person.

Anyone observing me would have thought my life was very satisfactory. I had a secure and interesting job with a good salary. I was married and had two young daughters. We lived a comfortable life in a new house in South Wales, in pleasant surroundings near both the countryside and the sea. I enjoyed good music, the theatre, and literature. And yet, I felt that something was missing. I had a vague sense of being *unfulfilled* at some level of my being.

In addition to my research work, I found myself thinking about problems of a more general nature. I found time to think, particularly during the long summer vacations. I had, of course, been trained to use my brain to think when I was an undergraduate at the University, as well as through my more recent work as a lecturer. As a mathematician, I had been trained to formulate solutions to problems logically. But one question in particular proved difficult to answer: Why did I feel this basic sense of discontent?

From both material and intellectual points of view, my life was very satisfactory—*ideal*, even. It seemed to me that my problem must involve my life at its deepest level. Perhaps it was my study of the levels of the brain that had prompted this deep concern.

At that time, too, I began to develop a friendship with a neighbor who was a Christian. He

and I would discuss many things together. I always provided the "rational" approach, in contrast to his more spiritual explanations. I enjoyed
these good-natured conversations. In particular,
I prided myself on what I thought was the in-
cisive attack of pure logic that, to my mind, cut
right through all the "supernatural" arguments
of my friend.

I think it must have been about that time that
my neighbor directed my attention to the third
chapter of the gospel of John. Here I read about
the classic confrontation between Jesus and Nicodemus, who was one of the civic and religious
leaders in Jerusalem during Jesus' time. Nicodemus was a great thinker—a learned theologian
of the classic Jewish mold. Jesus was very different. He was a dynamic young leader, just beginning to spread a new theology. He proclaimed
the startling news that, because of God's love for
the world, He—being God's own Son—had been
sent to bring salvation and new life to men. *Could
that message have any significance for me?* I wondered.

I began to think about the way that scientific
thinking has advanced through the centuries.
Man has always sought after *truth*. He has always
wanted to increase his knowledge of the natural
world. He has never been content to remain
within existing, flawed, spheres of knowledge.
In every branch of science, earlier ideas have
been modified or changed. I thought of the way
in which Copernicus advanced astronomy because he refused to accept the Ptolemaeic view
of the universe. I reflected on the dramatic way

that Einstein's theories had burst through the confines of Newtonian physics. Yet, as I thought about our many innovations, it became clear to me that even our best systems of scientific truth still suffer from distinct limitations. They provide answers to *some* questions, but they never answer *all* of them.

One thing concerned me most of all. As a scientist, I knew that to cling to old or partial theories when superior ones exist would be to stunt the growth of science and to limit one's own involvement in its advance. With that in mind, I began to wonder whether my denial of the very existence of a spiritual realm had been logical and wise. Our understanding of the workings of the brain is still very incomplete. We know all too little of the stimuli to which it responds.

Carefully I examined the biblical account of the conversation between Jesus and Nicodemus. Nicodemus had wanted to know how Jesus could do the amazing things that He did. Jesus replied that there was *only one way* in which anyone could understand the sovereign power of God: that person must be "born again." Clearly, Nicodemus had even more difficulty understanding this than we do. I realized that the need to be born in this way—"born of the Spirit [of God]," as the Bible puts it (John 3:6)—might well be a clue to the solution of my own problem, too.

As I continued to search for the basic truths of spiritual life, I learned that in order to enter it, a person has to be deeply penitent and to deeply regret the years in which he has lived independently of God. I discovered that if I came to Him in faith and believed He would act to help me, He would do so out of love for me, irrespective of anything I had previously done. Only then could I become fully alive. Only then would I begin to grow spiritually.

I sensed that the only way I could break out of my state of chronic discontent was to put those theories to the test. It was then that I began to pray that I might be helped to know God as my neighbor clearly did.

Little did I realize at that time that the answer to my prayer was to mean entry to a whole new life—spiritual life! If my basic problem was deep-rooted and difficult to understand, then the solution to it needed to be deeply penetrating and complete. And so it was! I soon discovered that acknowledging Jesus Christ as Lord of my life— and becoming alive in His Spirit—was to initiate a complete renewal of my existence from the deepest level up. I now realize that my previous unease had resulted from an awareness of an innate deadness that could be reinvigorated by God alone. I had needed to be born again.

How do I understand the new birth today? Let me put it this way: The physical life is material and tangible—recognizable by the five senses. The spiritual life is not directly detectable by those five senses, yet it is just as real—in the same way that the mind is as real as the brain. Indeed, the spiritual life is by far the more enduring of the two; the Bible asserts that it is "life everlasting." I have discovered that the love, joy, and peace that the spiritual life brings far surpass the fruits of mere physical existence. I have begun to understand what Jesus meant when he said, "I have come that [you] might have life, and might have it more abundantly" (John 10:10).

As a scientist, I am certain that to cling to the old or partial theories, when better and more complete ones exist, is to slow down the growth and progress of science. The scientist hopes to come closer to the full truth of the physical world, based upon conclusions drawn from his research. Similarly, I have to conclude that to deny the existence of God is to reject new, better, and more complete knowledge about ourselves, life, and the universe we live in.

To refuse to accept the revealed deity of Jesus Christ—and the spiritual life God offers us through faith in Him—is to stagnate in a state of spiritual morbidity. Such a refusal would mean confinement to a material world, whose matter is transient and whose values are short-lived in the extreme. To be imprisoned voluntarily in such an existence is to be deliberately blind to the liberating truth that leads to everlasting life.

As a scientist, I look for scientific "truth" in my research, knowing that such truth is transitory. It may be superceded or refuted at any time. But, since I am a Christian, my life and work are now based on the most comprehensive and unequivocal statement ever made about truth: Jesus Christ once said, "*I am* the truth" (John 14:6, italics added).

All the truth of the universe is to be found in Him.

The trouble with this truth is that it defies

ordinary definition and discovery. It transcends the logic of the scientist, the persuasive speeches of the politician, and the deepest reasoning of the atheist or agnostic philosopher. The only way of access to it is through the "new birth," through faith in Jesus Christ. It was by trusting Him that I found the fulfillment I had previously lacked.

Today I know that I have found *eternal* truth in Jesus Christ, who said to those around Him, "You shall know the truth, and the truth shall make you free" (John 8:32).

10

Beyond Einstein

It takes three hundred tons of detection equipment to confirm that a millionth-billionth-inch proton has arrived.

In the high-energy world of Fermilab, *Dr. Randall J. Fisk* sees God's "displayed excellence" at the sub-atomic level.

Randall J. Fisk *received his Ph.D. in High Energy Physics from the State University of New York (SUNY) at Stony Brook. He worked from 1978 to 1981 at one of the world's largest elementary particle research facilities, the Fermi National Accelerator Laboratory (Fermilab), in Batavia, Illinois.*

Dr. Fisk now teaches physics at Valparaiso (Ind.) University.

I am a physicist whose field of study has been elementary particle physics. I have studied the very smallest building blocks of the universe: the particles of which atoms are made.

To study particles so small, we used Fermilab's huge proton accelerator, which accelerated protons to an energy of almost half a trillion electron volts, in an underground ring more than one mile in diameter. As the rapidly-moving protons slammed into metal targets, they would break apart, enabling us to discover what protons are made of and what forces hold them together. In this way, we have studied a world measured in millionths of billionths of an inch!

What is the universe like when we look at it from that vantage point? To a scientist, it's beautiful! The scientific laws governing the sub-atomic world are stunning in their simplicity. The particles and forces operate in their strange and amazing ways, and when billions of billions of billions of them are put together, we have the beautiful large-scale world in which we live.

When I stare into a clear, star-filled sky, or contemplate the sub-atomic world, or look at a beautiful sunset, I have to agree with the psalmist David: "The heavens are telling of the glory of God; And their expanse is declaring the work of

His hands" (Psalm 19:1). Someone once defined the glory of God as "God's displayed excellence." God is excellent in everything He does, and His creation displays it.

The nuclear particles that I have studied are just the building blocks that God used in making everything that exists. The beauty of our world reflects the excellence of Him who created those infinitesimal particles, and who then formed them into everything we see around us.

Just *discovering* some of the sub-atomic complexities has earned scientists Nobel Prizes. What greater honor belongs to the One who *created* those complexities!

The beauty of God's creation is more than just skin-deep. His glory—His displayed excellence—is evident no matter how close or how far away you look at it. From outer space, Earth looks like a blue-and-white gem, sparkling in the sun. On Earth, the beauty of a flower or a mountain stream amazes us.

And very close up, I can attest that the universe has a unique beauty all its own. God's world is beautiful through and through.

Albert Einstein was overwhelmed with the simple beauty he found in the equations governing relativity—a symmetry and order that he called "elegance." It seemed to him that there had to be a Creator, and an awe-inspiring one at that. Sadly, however, Einstein couldn't believe a God so big and so majestic as to have created the universe would really care about him personally.

In that respect, I've gone beyond Einstein. I've

discovered that the true and living God is concerned about me—and that He knows each of
us by name.

Indeed, no thought I have ever pondered in
the thought-provoking field of physics has stag-
gered me more than this: Looking at the mul-
titude of stars on a clear night, I know that the
Creator of it all knows and loves me!

Let me tell you a story. I've been talking about
the excellence and care God took in creating the
universe. But that isn't God's specialty; it is not
his *highest* glory. God's excellence is best displayed in his *love*. As I have grown to appreciate
the excellent way that God's universe is made, I
have even more learned to appreciate the excellent elegance of His love.

God's display of excellence in love can be
found in the person and mission of Jesus
Christ—the ultimate in love. The more closely I
have looked at the Bible, the more I have observed that every act of Jesus was motivated by
undiluted love. Jesus Christ never had a selfish
thought. His entire life was based on helping
others. He willingly experienced a death more
agonizing than we can ever know, so that we
could have eternal life and a relationship with
God like that of children with their loving father.

Jesus portrayed God as standing with His arms
outstretched, inviting people to embrace Him.
Only the infinite God could have infinite love—
love inclusive enough to contain every person
who accepts His "whosoever" invitation.

For a long time I had been searching for the

truth. I went into physics to see what truth was there. I was dissatisfied with the idea that there was no God. I simply could not believe that a world so beautiful was the result of chance occurrences. The idea that my own being could have been nothing more than a meaningless accident also sounded very unlikely.

I examined several religions, but I found them unsatisfying.

Conversations with a secretary in the physics department at Fermilab stimulated me to take a serious look at Christianity. Until then I had considered Jesus only a great philosopher and a very spiritual man. A neighbor held an information class, and I began to learn what Jesus was really all about. Eventually, I married the secretary who had helped me to consider Christ.

I didn't understand why at the time, but I had a real hunger to read about Jesus in the Bible. I was having an intellectual battle. Logically and historically, the good news of Jesus seemed very probably true. But can we ever really *know* what is the truth? First Corinthians 2:14 says that the natural mind cannot understand the things of God; they must be discerned by spiritual perception.

When I continued reading God's Word, something inside me resonated in response, telling me that what I was reading was true. I can't point to a specific moment of salvation; it probably occurred when God worked faith in my heart by telling me that what I was reading in the Bible was true.

My work in physics provides an analogy. I experimented with the *neutrino*, a peculiar type of elementary particle that can pass right through the Earth and come out of the other side. Unless you have the right equipment to detect neutrinos, you'll never know they are there. In fact, fifty years ago no one knew they existed.

Even today, detecting them requires a three-hundred-ton "flash tube detector." Out of the trillions of neutrinos in our beam, a few happen to hit the detector—composed of several hundred thousand neon tubes primed for the experiment, energized with high voltage, and on the brink of glowing. If a charged particle strikes a tube, the tube glows to report the passage, revealing exactly where it occurred.

Just because neutrinos can't be detected with our five senses doesn't mean that they aren't there. Intricate, sensitive equipment confirms that neutrinos exist. It takes something special to detect them.

In the same way, using only our natural mind and five senses, we can't discover the reality of God's truth. I don't think God *wants* us to discover His truth with our senses; otherwise we would claim it as *our* discovery, and the beauty of it all would be destroyed. God wants to provide us with His truth as a gift, because He loves us.

God was enabling me to experience the truth that I was learning in that Bible class. In other words, God was giving me the very salvation I was learning about, by creating in me the faith necessary to receive it. I remember how the reality of it hit me forcibly one day. I came upon a large gathering of Christians praising and worshiping the Lord. Within my spirit, I felt God's Spirit rejoicing. I cried, because I had never felt such a deep, genuine beauty.

I felt the love of God, and I knew that same love had indeed sent Jesus to the earth. I sensed the joy and peace of knowing it was all true and real. I suddenly realized that God loved me so intensely that I could actually call Him my Father. I began to know Jesus personally as my friend and Lord, instead of just knowing about Him.

The excellence of God, which I had seen in the universe around me, now engulfed me. I tasted and shared in an even more excellent excellence: His love and His presence.

Yes, the grandeur of God is surely found in His creation—in the sub-atomic world, in the heavens, and in nature. But unless we find the glory of God in His love and presence, we will miss His very best.

The innermost desire of my heart now is to experience more of this glory. David says it so beautifully:

> One thing have I desired of the Lord,
> that will I seek after;
> that I may dwell in the house of the Lord
> all the days of my life,
> to behold the beauty of the Lord,
> and to inquire in His temple.
>
> (Psalm 27:4)

The world of elementary particle physics has made me appreciate God as the brilliantly intelligent and powerful Creator. Personal *contact* with Him shows me what a *loving* God He is.

11

The God Who Couldn't Be Hidden

Grow up in an atheistic country, attending atheistic schools and living with atheistic parents, and sociological theory says you'll grow up an atheist.

But even in an environment so well "shielded" from God, *Alexander Semyonov* found God. As he studied architecture, he observed that nature possessed an impressive combination of form and function that showed a Great Architect behind it. Even atheistic books helped him to learn more about the true nature of the God they denounced as false. A godly neighbor and Christian radio broadcasts represented other influences from which he couldn't be "protected."

A young Russian relates his story.

Alexander Semyonov, *a native of the Soviet Union, counts architecture and art as his main interests. During his course of studies in college, he made a public profession of faith in Christ and subsequently joined a Baptist church. His name has been changed to preserve anonymity.*

"**B**eing determines consciousness," some philosophers have taught. The idea contains an element of truth: Our surroundings help to shape our views and attitudes toward life. However, materialists often suppose that our minds are *nothing more* than reflections of our environment. To control the situation in which a person lives, they say, is to control what that person becomes.

We have to ask ourselves, however: Are the creations of designers and engineers really reflections of phenomena already existing in the world? Or does a mind create something that had not existed before?

How do we explain the construction of entirely new machinery and equipment, or the development of previously unheard-of synthetic materials by modern chemists? Can a symphony newly born in the mind of a composer, or an original design arising in the consciousness of an architect, be attributed simply to the influences of the material environment?

Also, is it not well documented that various people have quite different reactions to identical external stimuli and will perceive the same information differently?

Consciousness and man's spiritual world are

much more complex than certain materialists present them to be. The Bible points out that belief in God and the Christian world view are not necessarily the result of education or of the long-term influence of one group of people on another. God is able to draw to Himself disparate people, living in the most diverse places, having varied cultural and educational backgrounds. "For whom He foreknew, He also predestined to become conformed to the image of His Son, . . .and whom He predestined, these He also called; and whom He called, these He also justified . . ." we read in Paul's epistle to the Romans (8:29-30).

In our modern day and age also, there are those who respond affirmatively to God's call. These are people of various nationalities, residents of various countries, attending a variety of churches, but together they constitute God's chosen people, the universal church of Christ, about which the apostle Paul wrote, "[God] chose us in Him before the foundation of the world, that we should be blameless and holy before Him. In love He predestined us to adoption as sons through Jesus Christ to Himself . . ." (Ephesians 1:4-5). "Who shall separate us from the love of Christ? Shall tribulation, or distress, or persecution, or famine, or nakedness, or peril, or sword? . . .In all these things we overwhelmingly conquer through Him who loved us" (Romans 8:35, 37). It is to this group of people that I also belong. And it was in the Soviet Union, an atheistic country, that God chose to call me to His life of faith.

In the Soviet Union, atheism is inculcated from the primary grades through the university level. Radio, television, and the printed word are often used for atheistic propaganda, of which the fundamental thesis is: "Science refutes religious delusion." Bibles and Christian literature are not sold in stores and are not made available in public libraries. On the other hand, bookstores and libraries offer a plethora of atheistic materials, whose authors undertake to convince the reader that religious convictions are untenable.

The overwhelming majority of the population of the Soviet Union does not believe in God. My parents, both of whom have advanced degrees, are also in that number. Yet, despite the fact that I was raised in an atheistic society and by atheistic parents, a religious outlook developed in my consciousness. I became a Christian, and God is helping me to stand firm in my faith.

How was it that I learned about God and the teaching of Christ? The Bible reveals that God can bear witness to Himself in diverse ways, using different people and different circumstances.

My first encounter with God came through conversations with an elderly lady who lived next door to us. This woman loved children. When I was still a child, she would often invite me in for a visit, a snack, and sometimes even a little gift.

It was in her home that I first came upon a painting depicting the crucifixion of Christ. As far as I can remember, it was an antique black-and-white silk reproduction of a painting by one of the masters of the Italian Renaissance. I was captivated by the picture and began to ask my neighbor questions about it. She explained to me who was depicted in the picture, and that He sees and knows all the affairs of men. Because of her love, her witness left a lasting imprint on my soul.

In the letter of Paul to the Romans, we read this about God the Creator: "Since the creation of the world His invisible attributes, His eternal power and divine nature, have been clearly seen, being understood through what has been made . . ." (1:20). I believe that the created world bore witness to me of its Maker. The beauty of nature, its multiformity and complexity, unceasingly proclaim the wisdom of its Creator. And, although we find negative aspects in nature (which the Bible explains as the consequence of man's sin), it still continues to arouse our admiration and delight.

My parents instilled in me a love of nature from early childhood. We would often ride off to the forest, go hiking, and take kayak trips. In the winter we would go cross-country skiing. I remember how my mother would always direct my attention to the beauty of wooded scenery.

At the same time, my parents developed in me a love for art. Although their professional work had little in common with the arts, they cultivated a strong interest and included me in their frequent visits to art galleries and exhibits. There I compared the painted landscapes with the scenes I saw in nature. *Famous artists, in creating such marvelous paintings, studied in nature's school,*

I reflected. *But who was the Great Artist that created nature?*

Later, when I pursued a vocation in architecture and studied it in college, I would sometimes compare forms and structures existing in nature with the forms and structures devised by architects. Durability, utility of form, and beauty are the requisite properties of good architecture. And these properties are evident in living nature. It is not surprising that the famous scientist Galileo Galilei devised a formula used by engineers in suspending girders—after having analyzed the durable design of plant stems! It is also well known that Brunelesci, the great architect of the Italian Renaissance, used the shell of a bird's egg as his model for the famous Florentine Cathedral. Today, architects and engineers frequently adopt the honeycomb in their designs to insure both economy and durability.

Throughout the centuries, stylized forms of living have also been used in architectural ornamentation. And architects have tried to make their designs harmonize with the surrounding natural environment. My studies in architecture have helped me to better understand and appreciate the creations of the great architects. It is difficult to create beauty, to create something pleasing to behold and perfect in form.

Beauty in every true work of architecture and art is the harmony of all its parts and, simultaneously, the absence of dull monotony. It is the exquisite combination of form, line, and color. Beauty, in a matter of speaking, is the complex order present in the works of art and architecture. We revere the great masters, who were able to create this unique order; we praise their talent and their wisdom. But the beauty of man-made creations often pales before the beauty of nature. Could the creation of beauty in nature possibly have come about without genius or ability? We know that nothing complex or beautiful can be created without an intellect. Who, then, created the beauty and design found in nature?

These kinds of reflections led me to the idea of a Supreme Intellect, or a "Great Architect," who created nature. The idea of God the Creator was far more logical to me than the materialistic claim that everything came about by itself as a result of chance.

I remember coming across a pre-revolutionary edition of the collected essays of the distinguished Russian scientist Mikhail Lomonosov. In one of them he wrote:

> The Creator gave the human race two books. In one He revealed His majesty, in the other—His will. The first is the visible world, which He created so that man—beholding the magnitude, the beauty, and the harmony of His creation—could acknowledge God's omnipotence. The second book is Holy Scripture.

Initially God revealed Himself to me through the first book, and later through the second.

I believe that God also reminded me of Himself every time I listened to classical music with a religious theme, or viewed religious works of art. I also had the opportunity to learn more about God and Christian ethics from the works of Russian classical literature. Christianity exerted an obvious influence on the works of the prominent Russian writers of the nineteenth century. Christian love and compassion are reflected in the literature of that period, such as the works of Tolstoy and Dostoevsky. For example, Dostoevsky's characteristic theme describes and analyzes the acute dramatic situations of human life from a Christian perspective. His books provided me with basic Christian instruction.

At times I would try to initiate a discussion with my friends and relatives on some religio-philosophical topic. But no one seemed to share my views about God. "Atheistic literature has completely refuted your ideas," they claimed. In my case, however strange it may sound, atheistic books only broadened my understanding of the Christian faith.

I read atheistic literature because I was interested in the opposite; I wanted to verify my views that God *did* exist. And the materials I read could not give me a single argument sufficient to undermine my convictions. The books included, in one form or another, many theological concepts—given for the sole purpose of criticizing them. The authors of atheistic materials are obliged to quote the ideas of theologians, because it is quite difficult for the Soviet reader to become otherwise acquainted with them. Sometimes such books, before proceeding to criticize religion, quote from the Bible or give facts about the history of the church. Thus, by reading atheistic propaganda, I was able to gain a better understanding of Christian thought.

My religious quest was further advanced by Christian radio programs that were broadcast from other countries. Such programs represent one of the few sources to which Russian believers can turn in order to learn about God. The broadcasts are of special significance, for as we read in Romans 10:17, "Faith comes from hearing, and hearing by the Word of Christ."

In order to find like-minded individuals who shared my views, I began to visit various places of worship. I went to Orthodox churches, the synagogue, and the Baptist church, where I became close to the Christian young people. At the Baptist church, I was able to get a Bible, and, as I read it, I realized why this extraordinary ancient book was the source of inspiration for so many people.

From time to time I would pray to God, especially in difficult situations. But the day finally arrived when I turned to God in prayer with all my heart. I repented of my sins and by faith accepted Jesus Christ as my Savior, dedicating my entire life to God from that moment on. About a year later, I was baptized in the Baptist church.

Joining the local church has tremendous scriptural significance, but more importantly, at the moment of my decision I became a member of the universal body of Christ, a part of God's chosen people. The Scriptures say that Christ ". . . gave Himself for us, that He might redeem us from every lawless deed and purify for Himself a people for His own possession, zealous for good deeds" (Titus 1:14).

My decision to live according to the principles of the Christian faith has puzzled my non-Christian friends. They consider life in Christ to be weird and useless zealotry, somewhat akin to the quest of Cervantes's Don Quixote. Living a Christian life, however, means being involved in the real world—resisting evil and actively promoting good.

I believe that a life lived more honestly and kindly is richer for the individual living it. In fact, I believe that if *everyone* obeyed the commandments of Christ, the life of *all of society* would be improved. After all, that is the plan of the Master Designer.

12

Moon Man in Moscow

Two totally dissimilar searches preoccupy the minds of many American and Soviet citizens today. One is man's exploration of space; the other is each person's own quest for God.

In June 1979, an American astronaut brought the two searches together during a unique presentation in the Soviet Union. *Colonel James B. Irwin*, pilot of the Lunar Module on the Apollo 15 flight, spoke of his experiences on the moon and how he found God obviously present there. Speaking to a packed congregation in the Evangelical Christian-Baptist Church in Moscow, Jim told how that especially close encounter with God changed the whole course of his subsequent life.

This condensation of his Moscow message has been prepared from a transcript of the talk he gave, reprinted in the official Russian-Baptist journal, *Bratski Vestnik* (Fraternal Messenger).

Colonel James B. Irwin *is one of twelve humans ever to have walked on the surface of the moon. As Lunar Module Pilot of the Apollo 15 mission, he lifted off from Cape Kennedy on July 26, 1971, and landed on the moon four days later for a record sixty-seven hour stay there.*

"I had been so absorbed in preparing for the scientific *flight that it never even occurred to me how high the* spiritual *flight could be," Irwin says. While on the lunar surface, he became more aware of God than he had been for years. He retired from NASA in 1972 to found High Flight Foundation, an evangelistic organization based in Colorado Springs, Colorado. His lectures about his lunar experiences and his faith have taken him more than a million miles—double the distance he traveled round-trip to the moon!*

"I'm a guy who's had a unique experience that I would like to share," Irwin says. "It was the greatest trip I'll ever make, and since all the people paid for it, I feel they deserve a personal trip report. That's what I'm giving them now."

I will speak today as a person who has had an opportunity to accomplish a *long journey* from our planet, Earth, to the moon. The Bible tells us about the sun and the moon in the book of Genesis.

> God made the two great lights, the greater light to govern the day, and the lesser light to govern the night: He made the stars also. (1:16)

When I was a boy, the moon held a great fascination for me, and for some reason or another, I surely hoped to fly there someday. I later regretted talking about the idea to my friends and relatives, because they made fun of me for it. Consequently, I kept quiet about it from then on, but secretly I believed and dreamed about it all the same.

I was born into a family in which both my mother and my father knew God. I learned about Jesus Christ from my mother, and I am grateful to her for this. I will never forget the day when I first visited an Evangelical Baptist church. God Himself seemed to say: "Now it's your turn. I want to enter your life and fill it with Myself."

So I turned to the Lord, and He began controlling my life in His all-wise and loving way. I didn't know where the Lord would lead me, but my only desire was that it would be *upwards!*

However, there were also setbacks in my life. I loved airplanes very much, so I joined the US Air Force. With time, I gained a lot of experience. I flew various planes, and I flew higher and faster than anyone had previously flown. But at that time I strayed from the spiritual life.

Soon I experienced a misfortune. Together with a friend, I had a wreck. Our plane crashed, but by some miracle, it did not explode. Both of my legs were fractured, and my jaw was broken. The doctors wanted to amputate my right leg. When I regained consciousness, I could not understand how such a thing could have happened to me—Jim Irwin, the super-pilot!

Then I remembered God and began to pray: "Lord, why did You lift me so high and then drop me so low?" I asked Him, "Are You trying to teach me something?" I really wanted an answer to that question. I also prayed for my recovery. And God answered my prayers. Four months later, I walked, healed, out of that hospital.

I wanted to fly again, but it was difficult to obtain permission from the Air Force authorities. In the end, they finally granted it to me, and I resumed my career in the air.

However, by then a new era had begun. Yuri Gagarin, a Russian cosmonaut, had paved the way into space. Soon Americans also had the opportunity to undertake space travel, and I applied to become an astronaut. I had to wait a long time, and I was right at the age limit by the time I was accepted. I had to study many new subjects and go through extensive training. I was preparing my body, mind, and spirit for journeys into space. Each day I prayed that God would help me in this effort.

After five years, in July 1971, three of us—Alfred Worden, David Scott, and myself—were prepared for the flight of Apollo 15 to the moon.

The hours passed slowly as we waited for the great day. But the last minutes flew by quickly, and finally—"all systems go!"—we felt the tremendous power of the rocket pressing us back into our seats. We were leaving Earth. The trip to the moon had begun. We counted on the fact that many people were praying for us—our families, our children, and our friends. We are thankful to all of those who prayed for us then.

After leaving Earth's orbit, when the ship had become parallel to Earth, we saw our dear planet through the window of the spacecraft. It passed by magnificently and triumphantly beneath us. The view of it was stunning. The earth was illuminated by the sun, and we could see the individual continents and countries. We were able to distinguish the reddish hues of the earth, the light-brown deserts and mountains, blue-green seas and oceans, and the white clouds.

However, as we set our course for the moon, the earth seemed to change noticeably in size. At first it had been the size of a melon, then it had shrunk to that of an orange. Finally, it hung like a pearl in the blackness of endless space. It was difficult to comprehend that this was the planet on which we lived. Everything that I loved, thought of, and cared about was located there below. I wondered how Earth's Creator Himself views our planet.

The farther we flew from Earth, the more I could sense the presence of Almighty God—His closeness and control. After three Earth days, David Scott and myself were able to land on the surface of the moon, while Al Worden continued to orbit around the moon.

In the lunar module "Falcon" we made our landing in the region of the Apennine mountain chain. Mountains surrounded us on three sides, while on the fourth, the eastern side, there was a big canyon, a deep ravine. My first feelings were connected with the mountains. I spontaneously recalled the words from Psalm 121:1-2: "I will lift up my eyes to the mountains; from whence shall my help come? My help comes from the LORD, who made heaven and earth."

The mountains, which were light brown in color, attracted our attention. It was a beautiful sunny morning, but much different from such a day on Earth, since there is no life on the moon.

As we were fulfilling our scientific mission, I felt a special closeness of God in everything, and I prayed to Him often. We had our difficulties, but the Lord helped us to overcome all of them. I sensed a kind of direct communication with God and felt His presence more than I had ever felt it on Earth. That was a real spiritual awakening for me. Since that time, God has given me a strong desire and compulsion to share my faith with others.

After three days, we set off for the return trip, and much was repeated in reverse order. But when our third parachute failed to open we returned to Earth a little earlier than the flight plan had anticipated. Naturally, our space capsule fell faster than it normally would have fallen. Our capsule came down on only two parachutes, right into the ocean. But we came through the whole thing safely, without any real problems.

Now I thank my God that I was able to visit the moon, as I had hoped to do even when I was a boy. I also thank Him that He helped us to return safely to Earth. I praise Him for giving me the opportunity to be His servant, and to be yours as well.

In closing, I would like to say to you all, *God lives!* He is on the moon as well as here on Earth. He is *everywhere*, wherever man may be. It was He who created the planet where we live. Earth is like a magnificent spaceship, completely in His care.

God loves us with an eternal love, which He proved to us in His Son, our Savior, Jesus Christ. Because He loved man, Christ died for each of us. He alone can forgive our sins and change our hearts. He is able to enter the life of each one of us and fill it with Himself. He gives strength to the weary and makes us victorious over death.

Jesus Himself is preparing all of us who know and love Him for a most distant journey—more distant even than the trip to the moon. The time will come when we will set out on this joyful way. The Lord wants us to be where He is throughout eternity.

13

Twenty-four Million Mile Man

"Astronauts are pretty ordinary people, when you get right down to it."

* * *

"Flying in space was a challenge I wanted to meet, to see if I could do it. The great part about it is accomplishing an objective—it's a gratifying feeling to get back on the ground and say, 'I made it!' "

* * *

"I became an astronaut by education, persistence, and the favor of a loving God."

* * *

"I have a very strong faith in God, and my relationship with Him is a very personal and close one. I rely on Him to direct my life. I find a great source of strength in my relationship with God. My faith in Him helps me in my day-to-day activities, and especially over some of the rougher spots in the space business."

"But God has His people in every walk of
life. If they are doing what He wants them to
do, that's what they ought to do—whether
they are astronauts, carpenters, teachers,
journalists, or whatever. That's where they're
going to shine best and be the most productive
Christians."

* * *

"It's natural to look up when you leave the
Earth, whether you're in an airplane or a
spacecraft. I think that there is a kind of call to
look toward God, but I don't think that it
should keep people down here from looking
toward Him as well. I now have a much greater
appreciation for the world that God has made,
the universe He has created. It's clear in my
mind that this would not have happened
by chance."

Colonel Jack Lousma

Colonel Jack Lousma *is best known for
his achievements as an American astronaut.
Born in Grand Rapids, Michigan, he
received his early education in Ann Arbor,
before obtaining a B.Sc. degree in aeronautical
engineering from the University of Michigan,
and the degree of Aeronautical Engineer
from the US Naval Postgraduate School in
1965.
After years of training—combined with
membership in the support crews for the Apollo*

9, 10, and 13 missions—Lousma was pilot of Skylab-3 from July to September 1973. He was then backup docking module pilot of the United States flight crew for the historic Apollo-Soyuz mission in 1975, in which the first American-Soviet link-up took place in space.

He has received numerous awards and honors in recognition of his service as a jet pilot and a NASA astronaut. These include: the US Navy Distinguished Service Medal, the City of Chicago Gold Medal, and an honorary doctorate in astronautical science from the University of Michigan.

Jack Lousma became a familiar figure in American living rooms during the first Space Shuttle launch in April 1981, when he appeared frequently on CBS-TV as NASA spokesman. He himself flew on the third Shuttle test flight in March 1982.

Col. Lousma retired from NASA in November 1983 and ran unsuccessfully for the U.S. Senate in 1984. He is now a free-lance consultant to aerospace companies.

Even after travelling 24,400,000 miles,* I really haven't gone anywhere. Each of the 858 orbits that I made in Skylab took ninety-three minutes. Light travels that far in less than one-seventh of a second!

God's universe is so massive, we don't even measure it in miles, but in light years. If we could travel at the speed of light for ten or fifteen billion years, we would probably get to the farthest thing from which we can receive signals. We realize that God has made a universe at least that large.

Cosmonauts Yuri Gagarin and Gherman Titov came back from Earth orbit to remark that they hadn't seen God anywhere in the heavens. They seemed to imply that they had explored most or all of the universe.

My experience in space gives me a different perspective on those claims. Moscow is farther from Leningrad than I was from Earth. Al Bean, Owen Garriott, and I orbited at the two hundred seventy-mile level, closer to Earth than Chicago is to Cleveland.

What fraction of the fifteen-billion light-year expanse of the universe have we explored? I as-

*39 million kilometers.

112

cended about one and one-half light-milliseconds. (Remember, a millisecond is a thousandth of a second.)

Even the men who walked on the moon were only 250,000 miles from Earth. When Mission Control ended a radio transmission to them, there was less than three seconds of silence before they heard an answer. It took nearly one and one-half seconds for the end of Houston's transmission to reach the moon, and the same again for the reply to begin arriving on Earth. Aren't we humans proud that we've penetrated that tiny fraction into the multiple-billion-light-year expanse of space? But we really haven't been anywhere yet, relatively speaking, because we must compare our travel to the size of God's infinite universe.

People say to me, "You've been to outer space, so you must have had a special religious experience. We would like to hear about it."

I answer them, "I'm sorry. My experience with God in space was no different than it was on Earth." Reading my Bible in Skylab was no different than reading it on Earth, as I had been doing daily for years.

The Bible does not say where heaven is. What it does tell us is that God lives everywhere. Indeed, in at least two places, Scripture records someone remarking to God, "Heaven and the highest heaven cannot contain Thee" (I Kings 8:27; 2 Chronicles 6:18). God cannot be confined in space.

The writer of the Psalms asks God, "Where can I go from Thy Spirit? Or where can I flee from Thy presence? If I ascend to heaven, Thou art there; If I make my bed in Sheol, behold, Thou art there" (Psalm 139:7-8).

Obviously, then, it's not our physical location that brings us to God—or takes us away from Him. Changing our astronomical position by a few light-seconds of distance has no effect on our relationship with God, who inhabits all of space. We can be as open or as closed to Him at sea level as we can in orbit. Our *altitude* is not the decisive factor, but our *attitude* is. Our own receptivity opens us to experiencing God's presence. Our refusal closes us to it. It's that simple.

God is as real to me on Earth as He was in space, and vice-versa. I have just as much opportunity to experience a relationship with God right here as I do in outer space.

We can see God on the small scale in the world around us. We can see Him on the large scale in the universe. But, most important, we can see Him in the effect He can have in our lives—within us.

Let's think of it this way, illustrated by a compass. The needle points north because there are magnetic lines of force around the world, stretching between a north and a south magnetic pole. We can't see those magnetic lines, but we can see their effects on our compass.

We need special equipment to detect the Earth's magnetic field. We're unaware of it unless we have a compass.

We also need special equipment to detect God's existence and influence. He tells us in the Bible, "The man without the Spirit does not accept the things that come from the Spirit of God, for they are foolishness to him, and he cannot understand them, because they are spiritually discerned" (1 Corinthians 2:14, *New International Version*).

As a compass must contain magnetic material to enable it to respond to magnetic forces, so we need God's nature in us to enable us to sense and respond to spiritual reality.

I pray daily to God, asking Him to guide me. I have seen Him directing my life into the various avenues and channels that have placed me where I am right now. I am confident that as I continue to ask Him to direct me, He will do so.

He has taken over in my family life, and I have a very strong and good family life. I have asked Him to watch over that and to guide it, and I can see Him doing so in the lives of my wife and my children. There are many, many examples that I could give, in which I have seen God answer prayer in my life and in the lives of my family members and other people I know. It's great to know that He cares for people's problems—even *my* problems and needs. He guides and directs my life, and, when I talk to Him, my prayers result in *answers*. He also speaks to us through His Word, the Bible, as well as through circumstances and other people.

When I was a youngster, I was very interested in airplanes. I took every opportunity to watch them take off. My father used to take me to the airport just to watch the planes take off and land, and to this day I still enjoy that. Even after all of my experience with airplanes, I still love to watch them take off and land.

I used to make model airplanes, and I recall that at an early age—when I was four or five years old—I even had the idea one day to try to build a small plane that would be powered by my mother's washing machine motor. Obviously, that didn't work out very well!

My ambitions began to be realized when I studied aeronautical engineering at the University of Michigan and graduated with my Bachelor of Science degree in 1959.

I had a strong desire to fly, so I became a pilot in the US Marines. When I got restless, I studied and earned a Master of Science degree. Then I began flying reconnaissance planes. When that began to lose its challenge, I prayed that God would guide me to something more fulfilling.

In 1965, the newspaper at the Marine base carried an announcement, saying, "Astronaut applications now being accepted." The notice listed the required qualifications and invited Marines who thought they might qualify to apply. So I applied—and waited. The odds against my being accepted were very great. Yet I was convinced that if God wanted me to be an astronaut, He would get me into the NASA program.

While my application was pending, the Marines reassigned me to Guantanamo Bay, Cuba. Every day, I went into the administration tent to ask if they had a message for me. Finally, after what seemed like a very long month, the message came. I was to go to Houston for interviews and testing. The competition was keen. After another long month, Al Shepard called with good news—I had been selected!

We moved to Houston with the distinct feeling that this was what God wanted us to do. NASA chose nineteen of us to train as astronauts. At first it seemed that my turn to fly in space would never come. I was on the support crew of the Apollo 9, 10, and 13 missions—becoming frustrated at not being on the flight crews. So my wife and I prayed about it a lot.

I would have liked to have gone to the moon. But, instead, a loving God has permitted me to fly nearly forty million kilometers in the Skylab mission. And God has provided another excellent alternative for me in the Space Shuttle. If I never go into space again, it will not really shake the world for me. What I have already learned about the universe has certainly enlarged my concept of God.

Remember the size of the universe, and how we measure it—not in terms of miles or kilometers, but in light years? I think that it is impossible to work in the field of space technology and exploration—to be acquainted with the magnitude and precision of space, and to be exposed to the principles of the universe—without being sure that it could not all have just happened by mere chance. It had to be engineered by a Master Planner and Designer. My work in the space program has *reinforced* my faith in God, the Creator.

But He is more than that. The Master Planner,

Creator of the universe, cares about each of us, specifically and personally.

On the one hand, we marvel at the immense size of the universe. On the other, God has made things so sub-microscopic that we can't even see them—the atom and its sub-components. He has made them with the same meticulous precision that He used in making the vast cosmos. In terms of size, human beings are between the size of a solar system and an atom. Would God skip us when He distributes His concern?

Logic says no. So does my personal experience with Him. He has demonstrated repeatedly that He is a God who cares not only about His great universe, but also about each of us individually, our daily needs, and our relationship to Him.

14

From One Heavenly Subject to Another

Why would a Ph.D. astrophysicist change career plans and become a seminary professor?

After the humorous rejoinder, "I switched from one heavenly subject to another," *Dr. Robert C. Newman* shares a tragedy that stimulated his thinking.

RADAS Director Dave Fisher interviewed Dr. Newman at the Annual Meeting of the American Scientific Affiliation, at Eastern College, in St. David's, Pennsylvania, during August 1981.

Dr. Robert C. Newman *has four degrees and is working on a fifth. He earned a B.S. in physics from Duke University, a Ph.D. in astrophysics from Cornell University, an M.Div. from Faith Theological Seminary, and an S.T.M. from Biblical School of Theology. He is currently a candidate for the Th.M. from Westminster Seminary.*

Moody Press readers know Dr. Newman as co-author (with the late Professor Peter Stoner) of the 1976 Moody Press revision of Science Speaks. *He is also co-author (with Herman J. Eckelmann, Jr. of* Genesis One and the Origin of the Earth *(Inter-Varsity Press, 1977).*

His professional activity has included a post-doctoral fellowship at the Bartol Research Foundation of the Franklin Institute in Swarthmore, Pennsylvania, and the position of associate professor of physics and mathematics at Shelton College in Cape May, New Jersey.

He is presently professor of New Testament at Biblical Theological Seminary in Hatfield, Pennsylvania, where he also teaches courses in apologetics and the interaction of science and Christianity. He also directs the Interdisciplinary Biblical Research Institute (IBRI), a Hatfield-based organization that schedules lectures and provides written and recorded material by a variety of speakers on scholarly Christian subjects.

Dr. Newman is a fellow of the American Scientific Affiliation and a member of the Evangelical Theological Society.

RADAS: Dr. Newman, what made you change from astrophysics to theology?

ROBERT NEWMAN: I merely switched from one heavenly subject to another! But, seriously, my scientific background helps my theological understanding and improves my ability to present a scientifically credible apologetic for God's existence.

One decisive factor in my career change was a tragic incident that occurred at a zoo. Just before I finished my doctoral program at Cornell, I attended a summer seminar on the dynamics of cosmic gases, held at the University of Wisconsin at Madison.

While I was relaxing at the Madison zoo, I saw a small child crawl over the outer barrier and approach the elephant cage. Thinking that the parents would protect the child, I kept walking. When I was about 150 feet (50 meters) away, the child climbed through the bars of the cage and was trampled to death.

That incident kept running through my mind. *Could I have saved the child? If I had shouted a warning, would he have listened to me? Did my failure to act cause his death?*

God used that event to convince me that I

needed to focus my career plans on a pursuit that was higher than studying the stars. If I went into astrophysics, I might be able to assist students with Christian matters on the side. But a lot of people might fail to hear the gospel message as a result of my pursuing a part-time ministry like that.

I wondered if there might be a more productive way of investing my life. Yes, it would certainly require additional years of study to become a theology professor. But then I would be able to train young people to become effective ministers, and I would also have the opportunity to speak at various colleges and universities and churches about the many scientific evidences that the Bible is indeed God's Word.

If I made astrophysics my career, I might make some minor contributions to the world's knowledge. But to turn people to salvation would be a more constructive way to spend my life.

RADAS: When you mention having studied in Cornell University's department of astronomy, many of us think of Dr. Carl Sagan. As host of the "Cosmos" television program, a best-selling author, and the subject of a *Time* magazine cover story, Sagan often presents viewpoints that specifically exclude God.

During your graduate studies at Cornell, were you exposed to any ideas that tested your biblical beliefs?

NEWMAN: I would say that Sagan's viewpoint is not unusual up there. He was not yet on the faculty during my student years, but the chairman of Cornell's astronomy department was Dr. Thomas Gold. In 1948, along with famed British astronomers Fred Hoyle and Hermann Bondi, Gold developed the "Steady-State" theory of the universe—the postulate that the universe had existed forever, without a beginning. That theory is very hard to reconcile with the statement of Genesis 1:1: "In the beginning God created the heavens and the earth."

Since that time, of course, data have been accumulating that lead to the opposite conclusion to what Gold, Hoyle, and Bondi had theorized. Current evidence points strongly to the conclusion that the universe had a definite beginning.

Gold was not as outspoken a critic of Christianity as Sagan is, but my professors would make statements now and then that would suggest that Christianity was outmoded. For example, often in our discussions of the history of science, they would emphasize the way that certain Christian views have impeded scientific progress—as in the case of Copernicus.

RADAS: Did their viewpoints shake your faith, even temporarily?

NEWMAN: No, largely because I had already learned to analyze various critical views of the Bible during my undergraduate days.

I grew up near Washington, D.C. My parents were believers, and my mother taught me a fair amount of Scripture in our home. During my boyhood, we went to a church that was biblically sound, although it became more liberal over the years.

At college, though, I became aware of a conflict in my mind over whether or not God had really spoken through the Bible. I had to take several required courses in religion, which raised questions that I didn't know how to answer. Contrary to what my parents had taught me, my professors were treating the Bible as a collection of the thoughts of men groping blindly after God, rather than as a true message from God Himself.

RADAS: How did you decide which position was right?

NEWMAN: In one such course, I began to notice that the explanation of certain passages of the Bible didn't fit the biblical data as well as the orthodox treatment of the matter did. I especially remember a passage in the book of Daniel. The liberal theologians taught that it was a prediction, referring to a time between Daniel and the Maccabean period.

But when I calculated the time information given in the passage, the liberal interpretation was in error by about a century. In contrast, if the command to rebuild the Temple referred to the time of Nehemiah, then the predictions compute correctly for the time of Jesus' birth as the Messiah. The orthodox interpretation seemed to hit the target with accuracy.

I was helped somewhat by coming into contact with the writings of C. S. Lewis—the first works

I had ever seen by an intellectual who was also a Christian. Lewis's work showed me that there were real answers to the questions that had raised problems in my mind.

I wasn't sure whether an intelligent person could actually believe in miracles. But Lewis helped me to see that just as we are able to act and make things happen that wouldn't otherwise take place, so God can create and manipulate events. For instance, if I lay a pen on the desk, it won't rise by itself into the air. But I can intervene and lift it.

The act of a human lifting a pen is "supernatural," in the sense that the inanimate parts of nature can't perform such an act. God can do things on an even higher plane than the works of humans. We define His "super-human" acts as miracles—humanly impossible feats that are within God's power to perform.

Perhaps even more important than noticing the contest between ideologies, I could see the *results* of the different viewpoints. The outworking of my professors' skepticism was a religion that had no *power*. My parents, on the other hand, had personal contact with Christ, who brought an undeniable change to a person's life.

RADAS: So Cornell Graduate School was not the first place you had to apply some real mental perspiration in deciding whether biblical Christianity made sense.

NEWMAN: Right. And when they started making an issue of the way certain Christian views have impeded scientific progress, it didn't take me long to discover the fact that wrong views of *any* subject impede progress.

Some professors quoted certain *outmoded* ways of understanding selected Bible passages, comparing them with *modern* theories of science and concluding that the Bible is ridiculous. But how can we compare twentieth-century science with sixteenth-century interpretations of the Bible? To assert that science is superior to the Bible, because current understandings of scientific phenomena are superior to obsolete interpretations of the Bible, is not accurate scholarship.

I'm convinced that the Bible is thoroughly trustworthy. But our understanding of it—especially of passages with scientific ramifications—is modified from century to century. The argument ought really to be between what can be fairly understood of what the Bible says on the basis of modern information, and atheistic constructions based on modern discoveries—comparing modern atheism with modern Christianity, not contrasting modern atheism with ancient Christianity.

RADAS: From your observation, would it be fair to say that the Bible itself has not impeded scientific progress, but that someone's *interpretation* of it sometimes has?

NEWMAN: Yes. Those of us who are trusting in Jesus are still human and fallible. Some of us

haven't been nearly careful enough to distinguish between the "thus saith the Lord" of revelation, and the "thus saith man" of interpretation.

RADAS: Besides discovering an intellectual con-
sistency in Christianity, was there any kind of felt
need that attracted you to Christ?

NEWMAN: Very early in life, I understood that
God was righteous and that I had displeased Him
and deserved punishment for not being good
enough. At age seven, I prayed with my parents'
pastor for God to forgive me.

However, I didn't understand the implications
of what I had done until I had deeper Bible
teaching while at Cornell. Herman Eckelmann,
Jr., had been a research associate at Cornell's
Center for Radiophysics and Space Research. At
the Faith Bible Church in Ithaca, New York, he
used his combined scientific and biblical education to help college students. Many of them
met God through his teaching. It was largely
through his example, along with that of seminary president Dr. Alan MacCrae, that I sensed
God's call to a similar type of teaching ministry.

I think I share another felt need with all of
mankind—the need to understand my place in
the universe, and to find fulfillment in it. I have
found that the Christianity of the Bible gives
satisfying answers to what life is all about and
the meaning of existence.

God has built a very complicated universe, and

He's built it in such a way that, if people want to go their own way, within certain limits they can do so. This universe is actually a moral testing ground.

RADAS: Are you implying that God is more than just the mighty Creator of the cosmos—that He takes a personal interest in each of His four-billion-plus creatures?

NEWMAN: God has demonstrated that fact in my life, educationally and vocationally. I chose my undergraduate college primarily because I could get financial aid there to pay my tuition. There had been some kind of mix-up, so I almost didn't get it. At the last minute they called me for an interview and granted me that scholarship.

Yet that college was an important influence on my eventual decision to teach at a seminary, because it raised criticism of the Bible to such a high level of importance in my mind that I had to answer detailed charges with detailed answers.

Attending Cornell for graduate study was just as providential. I wasn't even planning to send an application there originally. But my undergraduate advisor recommended that I should apply to several additional schools. Cornell, of course, was where Herman Eckelmann had such deep influence on my spiritual maturity and my career plans.

And, of course, there was that incident with the child at the zoo. Things like that don't happen very often. Yet I "happened" to be there at that tragic moment, and God used it to clinch my decision to teach for Him.

RADAS: I sometimes call events that seem providential, "coordinated coincidences." How would you repond to that?

NEWMAN: I like that phrase, in a tongue-in-cheek sort of way. If those pivotal events in my life were coincidental, they certainly coincided in striking ways.

I don't think that God expects every Christian astrophysicist to change careers. God has individualized guidance for each person.

In my case, my scientific background helps me to understand God's power and wisdom, and it enlarges my ability to present a scientifically credible apologetic for His existence. I'm convinced that the God who made the stars uses His mighty wisdom and power to guide each one of us into the career that is the most satisfying and the most constructive way of life.

15

Crossing Bridges

Imagine yourself in pressing danger with only one way to safety. You must go across a bridge whose construction is unfamiliar and whose strength seems suspect. How would you decide whether or not to take the risk and commit yourself to it?

John K. Holmes, when a science student majoring in mathematics and physics, was presented with this problem as an analogy to the spiritual dilemma he knew he was facing. Once it was resolved, he found that "quite remarkable things began to happen—as God began to answer prayer, my faith in Him grew steadily stronger."

Often that faith in God has been tested in John's life. As a young naval seaman, he found that he was the only Christian on his first ship. He has seen his faith tested in the lives of those he has met on his travels in many parts of the world as well.

As a representative for Inter-Varsity in Africa, he quickly realized that the Christian life was a daily battle for many native students, who were shunned by their peers or rejected by their relatives and friends. But he saw, too, the change that Jesus Christ worked in their lives, as they committed themselves fully to Him. He was encouraged that "many outstanding students, the best in Africa, shared the same experience of Jesus Christ" that he himself had had.

John says that it has been a real strengthening factor in his life to have been able to travel and work in other countries, amidst other cultures—and to know that "the bridge of faith is there for everyone in the world to cross!"

John K. Holmes *is Academic Dean of Stony Brook School, in Stony Brook, New York. He was born and brought up in southern England and received an M.A. in mathematics and physics from the University of Cambridge.*

He worked for many years in Africa, mainly at the University of Science and Technology, in Kumasi, Ghana, where he rose to the level of Senior Lecturer. He traveled widely throughout Africa as a representative for Inter-Varsity Christian Fellowship.

He published several scientific articles and was editor of SPAN *magazine, a Christian publication designed especially for the students in Africa. Today he is responsible for the educational and spiritual progress of four hundred boys and girls at a Christian boarding school in the northeastern corner of the United States.*

The solution to a single problem has changed my life. Let me tell you how it happened.

When I was in my last year of secondary school in Wimbledon, England, I was invited back to a summer sports camp. But one thing about going bothered me. I recalled that the first time I'd been invited, each of us had been asked to bring a Bible with him to the camp. I had not been brought up in a Christian home, and I had not understood why the Bible should be necessary at the camp. Nevertheless, I had found a dusty, old copy and taken it along with me. I had enjoyed the camp, but had been rather bored by the evening gatherings during which the Bible had been read and discussed. Those occasions had meant nothing to me at all.

Despite my reservations, I decided to go again. The games had been fun, and the other people were very sportsmanlike. This time I listened more carefully in the evening meetings. I began to feel that, whoever Jesus Christ was, *He seemed to have done something for me.* I felt badly about that, because I had ignored that possibility all my life.

My family had been quite opposed to the

Christian church. Once, my father had been secretary of a church sports club. Then, one day,
its treasurer—a leader in the church—had disappeared, taking the sports club funds with him!
*No wonder Dad brought us up to believe that all people
who went to church were hypocrites,* I had thought.
At our house, Sunday was a day of work in the
garden, followed by the best meal of the week.

But now, at camp, I began to think that perhaps I should not condemn *all* Christians, just
because of *one* man who had so clearly failed to
live as Christians should. I reminded myself that
I knew some believers whose lives surely pleased
God—if He was real.

I spoke to the camp leader. I told him that my
family would not be at all pleased if I announced
to them that I wanted to become a Christian
myself. After several long talks with different
people, I voiced my real objection: I could not
take the step of commitment to Christ because
I wasn't sure what would happen if I did! Perhaps God didn't exist at all; then I would have
upset my family for nothing.

At that time, I was studying physics and applied mathematics in preparation for my entry
to the university, and the counselor knew this.
So the crucial problem was posed: "Suppose you
were not sure about crossing a rather shaky-look-
ing bridge across a stream. What would you do
about it? Would you be *practical* about the matter,
or try to resolve it theoretically? Would you use
mathematics and physics, and sit down and try
to calculate the tensions and stresses in the

bridge—or would you put one foot on it, and then perhaps the other, to see if it would hold?"

"I guess it would depend on how badly I wanted to get across." I replied, after pondering the question for a few moments.

"Let's suppose it was a matter of life and death."

"Then I would *put one foot on the bridge!*" I decided.

My friend nodded. "Then, why don't you do that to find your way to God? Think of Jesus Christ as *the bridge*. You have nothing to lose. If this is all a myth and a fantasy, nothing will happen. You'll be no worse off than before. But if your step of faith is rewarded, it will have been well worth the try. Why not tell God that you are beginning to think He is real—that Jesus Christ might really have been His Son—and that you are beginning to want to trust Him with your life?"

Alone that night, I prayed a prayer that went something like this: "Oh, God, I'm not sure whether You exist or not—but if You do exist and sent Jesus Christ to be my Savior, then I want to trust Him and to come to know You for myself."

Immediately afterwards I didn't feel any different. But, over the next few weeks and months, as I put my faith into action, I began to see positive results. My family was convinced that my new interest was something that I would get over quickly, and did not seem unduly worried. However, as time passed, I became conscious that my faith was growing stronger. I realized that I was now *absolutely sure* that God was real; I had entered into a personal relationship with Him through trusting in His Son, Jesus Christ.

A few months later, I was called up for national service in the British military. I found myself drafted into the Royal Navy. My faith was tested during basic training on my first ship—as far as I knew, I was the only Christian believer on the entire crew. But reading the Bible helped me a lot. So, too, did meetings with other Christians while on shore leave. It was then that I met the wife of the Dean of RADAS. Gillian Barrett was then a small girl, who peeped around the top of the stairs to see who was coming to the Saturday night meetings held in her parents' home in Hinchley Wood, South London. Our next meeting was at a Christian conference in Gull Lake, Michigan, over thirty years later. It's because of that reunion that I am sharing my testimony with you today.

After four years of widespread travel in the Royal Navy, I went on to the University of Cambridge—one of Britain's top two universities—to study mathematics and physics. By then I enjoyed strong personal fellowship with God. And I had already been privileged to lead a number of other people to Him across the same bridge of faith that I had first crossed at the sports camp.

I worked in the United States for one year; there I met my wife. Then I taught for two years at St. Lawrence College in England. I had grown to appreciate, as a result of my travels, that the God I knew and loved could meet the needs of

every person throughout the world. Now I came to
see that He wanted me to spend more time sharing Him with others.

So, in 1954, I accepted a lectureship in mathematics and physics at the University of Science
and Technology in Kumasi, Ghana. In one hectic
period of only two years, I traveled to every university in that whole vast continent. My wife and
I spent fifteen years based there and in Kenya,
working with Inter-Varsity Christian Fellowship
and watching Christian groups grow in universities and colleges all over Africa.

The majority of advisors and helpers in those
groups have been professors in mathematics, science, and engineering. It is still true today that
wherever there is a strong engineering school
there is always a strong Christian witness as
well—I believe that is because engineers like
things that work!

I have met and worked with Christians not
only in America and Africa, but also in India,
Sri Lanka, Malta, Hong Kong, Singapore, Australia, and elsewhere in the Far East. I have
found that, whatever their language or the color
of their skin, those Christians have had experiences with God that are very much like my own.

Once while I was in Africa, a friend of mine
told me that he had been one of the first members of his tribe to trust in Christ. He came from
a totally different social environment from
mine—his educational background was practi-
cally zero. Yet I felt a closer affinity with him
than with the chairman of the university department in which I worked. That scientist, like

me, had come from England, and he had been to schools and universities very much like those I had attended. But he did not know God, and he could not understand our faith in Him. The believing tribesman knew and understood, and that made the difference in our friendship.

Some of my non-Christian colleagues in science have been amused by my Christian faith. Some of them have posed questions that have been difficult to answer. But my experience has indicated that there are far more difficult questions to answer for one who does not believe that God exists than there are for me.

As a college student, I was amazed by the order of the universe. Could all of this have come about by chance? How did life originate? And was there any purpose to it all? If there is no purpose to life, then our philosophy ought to be: "Eat, drink, and be merry; for tomorrow we die." But suppose, on the other hand, that there *is* a supreme Being who designed the universe and created man for His purposes. Then you and I must seek Him, and find His will for our lives.

It has been a great thrill for me to find that, at the other end of the bridge of faith, it is not only *God* who waits to welcome us, but also *a vast and varied company of other people who have crossed it, too.*

16

I'm a Missing Link

What started as a hobby for *David Fisher* is now a ministry that broadcasts in languages understood by more than a billion people.

The co-editor of this book, he has served at three of the stations of Trans World Radio (TWR), a six-million-watt missionary radio network covering 80 percent of the world's land area. While he was on an overseas assignment in 1971, a casual suggestion from a Hungarian colleague germinated into a burden for an outreach previously overlooked—and a series of "coordinated coincidences" contrived to make it possible.

David Fisher *earned his bachelor's degree in English from Roberts Wesleyan College, in Rochester, New York. Then he majored in missionary radio technology at Moody Bible Institute, from which he graduated in 1960. Subsequent to course work at the Institute of Slavic Studies, in Wheaton, Illinois, he completed his M.A. in inter-cultural missions at Wheaton College in 1985.*

Dave worked as Chief Engineer at a Christian radio station (WDAC, Lancaster, PA) from 1960 until 1963. In June 1963, he and his wife, Doris, and their family began work with Trans World Radio (TWR) in Monte Carlo, Monaco. This assignment was followed by others at the organization's stations in Swaziland, Africa, and on the Pacific island of Guam.

The Fishers have three children: Louise, who is now married and living in New Hampshire; Joy, who is working toward her doctorate in psychology at the University of Minnesota; and Paul, who is a college freshman studying computer science.

In 1978, Fisher requested TWR to place him "on loan" to meet a specialized programming need of the Slavic Gospel Association (SGA). He has become Director of the Radio Academy of Science (RADAS) broadcast, editing a program used jointly by SGA and TWR.

In addition to more than a thousand radio scripts, he has authored several dozen articles for Moody Monthly, Alliance Witness, Christian Reader, Evangelical Beacon, *and* Young Ambassador.

W hat would *you* do," the television announcer drooled in that commercially-saccharin tone of voice, "if you won five hundred dollars a week, for the rest of your life?"

I chuckled at the idea of entering the sweepstakes that he was advertising. But as I thought about his question, I answered with a response that surprised me. *"If I never had to earn another dollar in my life, I think I would do exactly what I'm doing now!"* I said to myself.

How did I get involved in such a fulfilling profession? Let's retrace pivotal points along the path.

"KEDVES HALLGATOINK" *(pronounced KAD-vesh HALL-guh-toe-ink)*, the Hungarian voice on the studio side of the soundproof glass began—*A strange-sounding way to greet his "dear listeners,"* I thought.

As I "rode gain" on the studio controls, the next several minutes were gibberish to me. But I knew that English made as little sense to the majority of the people in the world as Hungarian

did to me. That was why we Trans World Radio
(TWR) missionaries were broadcasting in sev-
enty-three languages. ("Whosoever" is a big
word!)

As the Hungarian speaker continued, I recalled the first time I had met Joe Steiner, the
slim six-footer whose resonant voice was stream-
ing from the monitor speaker. We had studied
together at Moody Bible Institute shortly after
he had left his homeland in 1956.

Joe was convinced that God wanted him to
prepare for some kind of Christian ministry. One
professor thought that Joe certainly had misread
God's guidance—that his heavily-accented English would hinder his preaching.

But the Lord had shown Joe why He wanted
him to speak Hungarian better than English. His
voice was passing through the faders under my
fingers, on the way to the ears of many of the
fifteen million Hungarian-speaking people in
Hungary and neighboring countries.

We often didn't stop at quitting time, because
Joe kept aiming for higher quality. After we
prayed about expanding our Hungarian music
library from the original eight songs, my family
and I spent three vacations recording 180 songs
in Hungary and Yugoslavia. Did God have to
answer our prayers by pointing His finger at the
people who called the need to His attention?

After a recording session in 1971, Joe didn't
leave the studio. His mouth unwound from its
troubled twist as he unburdened himself: "Dave,
we have a problem. Unbelievers aren't taking
seriously the things we're telling them. They've

been taught that the Bible is a man-made book, and that science has proved that God doesn't exist. What can we do?"

Prayer and discussion convinced us both that we needed to answer the objections of unbelievers and establish a more credible Christian witness in Hungary. After my assigned work each day, I went home to research suitable material—writing it in English for Joe to translate.

Soon Joe was enthusiastically telling broadcasters in other TWR departments about the scripts. Many of those people decided to translate them into their own languages.

The total number of people who could hear the program in their own languages passed the billion mark in 1978—as TWR's new Guam station began airing it to China in Mandarin and Cantonese. By that time, I had been transferred to Guam, where I was helping to get the new station on the air and being assigned increasing responsibilites.

One thing really puzzled me: While the scripts' outreach was growing, the amount of time available to research and write them properly was shrinking. Was God trying to tell me something?

A "coordinated coincidence" answered that question later that year. A missionary leader scanned the bulletin board of a church where he was a guest speaker. Peter Deyneka, Jr., General Director of the Slavic Gospel Association (SGA) in Wheaton, Illinois, spotted a letter from one of my fellow missionaries on Guam.

Reverend Deyneka read with interest that the new TWR station included Russian in its schedule. He dashed off a note, asking which parts of the vast eleven-time-zone width of the Soviet Union we were reaching, at what times of day, and with what letter response. The missionary who received the query passed it on to me to answer.

Peter's routine reply, "Thanks for the information," was accompanied by an enclosure. SGA's bi-monthly "Prayer and Praise" folder mentioned a plan to begin a new series of broadcasts for Soviet students and skeptics—the "Radio Academy of Science," or "RADAS" for short.

Was this the answer to my increasing burden to expand the writing side of my ministry? Or was it a temptation to get us off the track? My wife, Doris, and I prayed hard. Should we look into it? Hadn't God given us a life-long call to missionary radio at an overseas location? How could we know for sure?

To find out, I wrote to Reverend Deyneka, summarizing my past experience and enclosing sample scripts so that he could evaluate whether his need matched my ability to provide.

After sharing my letter with members of the SGA radio staff, he answered, "If you feel that the Lord is leading you, we'd be glad to have you join our team here in Wheaton."

God hadn't given anyone a visionary voice in the night. But along the trails of human channels, the footprints were unmistakably His.

Similar footprints on their side had led SGA to this expansion. Russian emigres had given some clues as missionaries witnessed to them in Europe and the U.S. After hearing the gospel for the first time, some would say, "My heart would like to believe, but my mind holds me back."

Asked to explain, they would invariably reveal some atheistic hang-up learned in Soviet science class: "Science has proven a hundred times that God doesn't exist." "The cosmonauts explored the heavens, and no god (always spelled with a small "g") was there." "The Bible says the earth was created in 4004 B.C., but science knows better." "The Bible is a man-made book, full of errors."

After showing them Moody Institute of Science films dubbed in Russian, SGA missionaries found emigres becoming open to the gospel. But what about the 260 million Soviets still living in the Soviet Union? Films couldn't reach them. What could?

A missionary observed, "People can put fences around their countries, but they can't put roofs over them." More than 90 percent of the radios in Russia can receive short-wave broadcasts from stations outside Soviet borders. Thousands of listeners had been saved since SGA pioneered Russian missionary broadcasts in 1941. *Based on emigre experience*, we wondered, *wouldn't even more respond if a new program could unravel this major hang-up, unwinding true science from the atheistic twists it has received in Soviet schools?*

A further nudge came when a British Christian professor of meteorology visited Monte Carlo. Joe Steiner struck again, telling Dr. Eric Barrett about the scripts I had been writing. Two years later, Eric spent a summer at SGA's International Headquarters in Wheaton, at Peter Dey-neka's request, laying the foundations for a wholly-new, magazine-style evangelistic program for Russia, based on science. By September 1977, he had compiled a 47-page manual describing the concept and giving samples of material to stimulate other scientists to write.

When Peter invited me to consider relocating in Wheaton, he enclosed a copy of that manual. As I read it, I wrote to him: "It looks as if God made two halves of the same plan—planting one of them in your heart and mind, and the other in mine."

In partial jest, I sometimes call myself "a missing link." Every previous assignment has prepared me for my present responsibility—giving me enough understanding of science to know what the Ph.D.'s are postulating in their polysyllables, yet keeping me enough of a layman to know how much to simplify or illustrate the material to make it understandable to the average listener.

Soviet students are taught to be skeptical of all religions and "holy books." So what happens when one of them suddenly discovers a broadcast that quotes extensively from the Bible? He has never seen a Bible for himself, and he has heard only negative comments about it. He regards it as being in the same league as "Alice in Wonderland!"

That's where our broadcast link comes in, providing facts that God uses to make Russian listeners more receptive to God. On a typical program, we present new evidence that the universe had a beginning—contrary to a favorite atheistic theory that matter had existed from eternity past and therefore didn't need a Creator. We strengthen the case by quoting Nobel Prize-winning scientists.

Then we point out that the new evidence agrees with statements in the Bible written thousands of years ago. The program concludes, "Maybe the Bible is more accurate than some of us have thought. Maybe it's worth researching just *how* accurate it really is!"

The skeptic suddenly finds himself listening with new respect to the biblical passages that follow.

People look up to astronauts, literally and figuratively. Russians still remember that pioneer cosmonauts Yuri Gagarin and Gherman Titov said in the 1960s that they didn't see God in space. Many Soviets consider those statements the final proof that God exists nowhere. How could we counter that?

We learned that astronaut Jack Lousma was a Christian. He provided us with testimonies that we translated and taped in time to be broadcast *while he was in orbit* on his flight of the Space Shuttle *Columbia*, March 22-30, 1982. (Punsters among us call his words "Apollo-getic statements.")

The on-air offer of Lousma's autographed picture, with Psalm 19:1 and his comment about what a large universe God had made, brought a record response from listeners.

Students in Russia must take courses in atheism, and every science class has an atheistic twist to it. The statement "Science has proved a hundred times that God does not exist" is repeated often in those lectures.

For years, listeners parroted that idea in letters to missionary radio stations—implying that broadcasters were wasting their time transmitting "religious superstition," because people were now too smart to believe it. Two years after RADAS went on the air, however, Monte Carlo Russian missionaries Nick and Rose Leonovich observed, "It's been more than a year since we've had a letter like that. RADAS is meeting a real need."

A former editor of the youth edition of *Pravda* listens to program cassettes, calls them "clear and convincing," and asks additional questions.

Christian emigres in West Germany find the program so useful in answering questions of their Russian compatriots that they dip deeply into their pockets to sponsor it on an additional station. At a weekly cost of several hundred dollars, this is the greatest vote of confidence listeners have given to any program in Russian broadcasting history.

Leaders of the Bible-believing churches in Russia ask every new convert who wants to be baptized to tell how he was saved. *Eighty percent* of them say that missionary radio was their first contact with genuine Christianity! Sometimes God uses radio alone to bring them to salvation. More often, He uses broadcasts to arouse interest in learning more from local Christians, who then lead them to conversion.

Nine stations now carry the program, using a

total power of three million watts to cover the entire Soviet Union adequately.

Christians involved in engineering, medicine, and the other sciences help with testimonies and subject suggestions and, occasionally, finished manuscripts. Members of the science faculty of Wheaton College have been especially helpful, inviting me to attend their weekly "S-cubed" sessions ("science sandwich seminars") and consulting on various script details.

As a student nearly everyone in our target countries has memorized the line "Science has proved a hundred times that God doesn't exist." We ask such people, "Oh, really? Can you name even ONE proof?" As they realize how hollow the anti-God statements are, we marshal solid pro-God arguments: "Here is abundant evidence that He does exist—and changed lives that can't be explained any other way."

It's frightening, yet fulfilling, to be that kind of link—frightening in the responsibility, yet fulfilling in the results. God has chosen me to be a conductor through whom He communicates to Russians and others who will never hear of Him except through their "leaky roof."

17

Medical Magellan of Pediatric Surgery

Dr. C. Everett Koop has been a pioneer in developing pediatric surgery from its "infancy" into a sophisticated life-saving science. Asked to name his most cherished honor, he cites the prestigious French Legion of Honor, presented to him by the speaker of the French Parliament in 1980—an award that eclipses his Gold Medals and other professional laurels.

The feat that brought him public fame, as the only surgeon known to have separated three sets of Siamese twins, is a logical outgrowth of his thirty-five-year career of spearheading a series of innovative surgical specialities. As Surgeon-in-Chief of Children's Hospital in Philadelphia, he established the world's first neonatal intensive care unit in 1962. Largely as a result, he says, "If we *lost* 90 percent of the babies with a particular defect twenty-five years ago, today we *save* 90 percent"—citing esophageal atresia, the absence of a normal esophageal opening, as a notable example.

As Professor of Pediatric Surgery at the University of Pennsylvania School of Medicine, he has trained many other surgeons, making similar life-saving skills available to communities throughout the world.

President Reagan appointed Dr. Koop to the post of US Surgeon General in 1981.

Dr. C. Everett Koop *is a Fellow of the American College of Surgeons and the American Academy of Pediatrics, and a member of more than a dozen medical societies throughout the world. He has served as president of the Surgical Section of the American Academy of Pediatric Surgery and of the American Pediatric Surgical Association.*

He was surgeon-in-chief of the Children's Hospital of Philadelphia during a distinguished thirty-five-year career. He also was Professor of Pediatric Surgery at the University of Pennsylvania School of Medicine.

Dr. Koop has been editor-in-chief of the Journal of Pediatric Surgery *and has served on editorial boards of counterpart publications in Germany and Japan.*

His writings on the popular level include The Right to Live; The Right to Die *(Tyndale, 1976);* Whatever Happened to the Human Race, *with Francis A. Schaeffer (Revell, 1979); and* Sometimes Mountains

Move, *with Mrs. Elizabeth Koop (Tyndale, 1979).*

RADAS Director Dave Fisher interviewed Dr. Koop in September 1979, on the Wheaton College campus in Illinois.

RADAS: Dr. Koop, your most publicized surgical procedure was the separation of the Rodriguez twins in 1974—Siamese twin baby girls. Will you please tell us a few things about that operation? Where were they joined?

DR. KOOP: Well, they looked as if they were sitting on each other's laps. These are called *ischiopagus* twins, which means that the bony pelvis that each should have had, in the form of a closed circle, was combined into one big open ellipse, instead.

The complications were that the urinary tract crossed from one child to the other, and the two children had only one colon, one rectum, and four vaginas. The liver was also a single organ, but one which could be divided.

RADAS: With so many serious abnormalities, were you able to achieve completely normal functioning in every respect?

KOOP: Yes. The remarkable thing is that this type of Siamese twinning had been treated surgically twice before; in both of those situations, one child did not come out very well. In one instance, one child was retarded; in the other, it developed a medical problem and failed to thrive. And in each instance, one of the twins had to have a permanent colostomy, a permanent artificial opening into the colon in place of a rectum.

The thing that is so great about the Rodriguez girls is that we finished up with two *absolutely complete and functioning females*. From the outside, except for some scars, they didn't look like anything other than normal children.

RADAS: Are there indications that, when they reach child-bearing age, they will be able to give birth?

KOOP: Well, that certainly was our expectation. But almost exactly three years after we operated upon them, Alta had a bean in her mouth, like a kidney bean. She inhaled it, and it went down her windpipe, and she strangled to death right on the spot. There was nothing really that could have been done, even if I had been standing right next to her.

But her surviving sister has finished kindergarten, will enter the first grade, and is to all intents and purposes just the same as any other six-year-old child.

RADAS: I understand that the operation took ten-and-a-half hours. What kind of surgical team was involved?

KOOP: Well, I was the captain of the ship, and I did the separation. Then I did the reparative work on the bowel in the two children. I had three assistants to help me on that, and we had a urologist and his assistant to take care of the urinary tract. We also had an orthopedist and his assistant to take care of some of the bony problems.

In addition to that, of course, we had four anesthesiologists—all doctors—and four nurses. So there were sixteen of us, all together.

I think one of the reasons that we were successful, not only in this separation but also in two other separations that we have done successfully, is that we had planned in advance what every person would do if anything went wrong. Something always does go wrong, and having such a large team always prepared to do the right thing at the right time got us through the procedure.

RADAS: How long was your planning session for a ten-and-a-half-hour operation involving sixteen people?

KOOP: Well, with the Rodriguez girls, we met every day for a week for about an hour at the end of the day, and we pooled our information. Then we sat down and talked it all over two days before the operation. We assigned the team members to their various tasks.

And then we did something I don't think most people do. We took the twins to the operating room and went through a dress rehearsal. We did everything except the operation.

That was a great help, because we learned a lot of things about the positioning on the table, what would happen after they were separated, how we could take care of the IV's, and so forth. So it was helpful to go through the rehearsal.

RADAS: You've received quite a cluster of awards and citations. Would you mind listing some of them?

KOOP: Well, I have been very fortunate to have been recognized by my colleagues all over the world. I have the highest award the British Association of Pediatric Surgeons can give, the Dennis Brown Gold Medal. I have the same thing from the American Academy of Pediatrics, the Ladd Medal.

Five universities* have given me honorary degrees—I suppose most of them stemming from what was considered to be my surgical expertise. And I am a member of surgical societies in Europe and in Asia as an honorary member—including Japan, Greece, France, Germany, Switzerland, and several other countries.

RADAS: Do you think that your Christian belief helps you in your surgical profession?

KOOP: Without any question. The things that I do deal with life and death. I often encounter the agony of parents separated from their children by death or facing difficult problems with malformation and long-term difficulties.

If I didn't believe that I had a God who was

*Dr. Koop has received honorary degrees from three additional universities since this interview was conducted.

solid and dependable, a God who makes no mistakes, I couldn't continue what I'm doing. I need that certainty to assure me that what I am doing is the right thing, and I need it in my day-to-day existence with all of the problems that I personally face. I would have a great deal of trouble with them if I didn't have complete faith in Jesus Christ.

I think that the hallmark of my existence is the integration of my surgical life with my Christian faith.

RADAS: You mentioned also that you had been through a traumatic personal experience. Would you mind sharing that with us, and telling us how God helped you through it?

KOOP: Well, my wife and I lost our twenty-year-old son in 1968. He was a very expert, technical mountain climber, and he was hit by an avalanche. Although still roped to his companion, he fell in such a way that he crashed into the face of the cliff like a pendulum and crushed his right knee and bled to death, some seven-hundred feet above the valley floor.

RADAS: That kind of news probably crushes a parent's spirit as traumatically as the actual accident crushes the son.

KOOP: Definitely. If it has never happened to you, you cannot understand it in any real way.

I had dealt with so many dying children all my life, that somehow or other I thought that the quantity of that experience would stand me in good stead when I had to go through something like that myself. But I can tell you that all the quantity in the world doesn't help you with the qualitative business of losing your own child.

Months in advance, the Lord had been preparing the family for David's death. In the fall of 1967, I went to Los Angeles to participate in a three-day graduate course in pediatric surgery. About five minutes before the close of the last session, someone from the floor asked the panel, "What do you tell the parents of a dying child?"

I told the panel faculty, "I'll take that," and I spoke extemporaneously for the remaining five minutes. Someone in the audience taped my remarks, and they were published in the *Medical Tribune*. A follow-up interview became the article "What I Tell a Dying Child's Parents" in the February 1968 issue of *Reader's Digest*.

Hundreds of letters arrived in response to that article—most of them from parents discussing the death of one of their own children. The amazing variety of reactions to death prepared us immeasurably as we agreed or disagreed with their viewpoints. In retrospect, we can see the hand of a loving Heavenly Father giving each of us what amounts to a course in philosophy on the dying child.

This was a time in the lives of those in my family when we simply leaned heavily on the wisdom and love of God. We believe that a person doesn't leave this earth one day earlier than the Lord decides.

We've had so many little evidences of the

things that God has accomplished in His world by taking our son that we feel, in a sense, *privileged* in God's planning for the kind of thing that we have seen happen. My wife and I have shared with our Christian friends in the form of a book entitled *Sometimes Mountains Move*. It is nothing more than an expression of the graciousness of God to us at the time of our greatest tragedy.

RADAS: What is the significance of the title, *Sometimes Mountains Move?*

KOOP: Our son didn't fall. He was hit by an avalanche. That's the unpredictable thing about mountain climbing. You can be the greatest expert in the world and never make a mistake, but you can't always predict what is going to happen to nature. When a mountain moves and you are in the way, there's nothing you can do about that.

RADAS: It moves you, too.

KOOP: It moves you, too. No question about that!

RADAS: Our interview is taking place while you and Dr. Francis Schaeffer are touring America with your film series *Whatever Happened to the Human Race?* In that film and in the book by the same title, you express strong opposition to the abortion-on-demand policies implemented following two key 1973 Supreme Court decisions.

Have your personal and professional encounters with death influenced you in forming your convictions about abortion?

KOOP: Definitely. There was a day when a thousand-gram (2.2 lb.) preemie had no chance for survival. Now it has a 50 percent chance, and newer techniques are saving even smaller ones.

As I said in *Whatever Happened to the Human Race?* part of American society has a schizophrenic mentality. We will transport a premature baby, who has a congenital defect incompatible with life, to a hospital a considerable distance away—so that a sophisticated team of doctors and nurses can correct that defect and plan for the rehabilitation of that youngster. Meanwhile, in a number of other hospitals within gunshot distance of that center, other medical personnel are destroying perfectly normal infants in the womb.

RADAS: The person who introduced you at today's luncheon here at Wheaton College alluded to something you tell the parents of children on whom you operate. What do you tell them?

KOOP: Well, you know many times parents tend to *idolize* the surgeon who actually performs the operative procedure on their child. When they are telling me what a wonderful guy I am to have done all these things for their child, I tell them that I was merely using the gifts that God gave me—and we both should be grateful to Him for the way in which the operation came out.

RADAS: In summary, what does God mean to you, in your daily life and in your scientific profession?

KOOP: Well, the fact that God is in control of this universe, as fallen as culture and civilization are, gives me a real reason to go on.

I never operate without having a subconscious feeling that there's no way this extraordinarily complicated mechanism known as the human body just happened to come up from slime and ooze someplace. When I make an incision with my scalpel, I see organs of such intricacy that there simply hasn't been enough time for natural evolutionary processes to have developed them.

The other thing that I would say is that the various abilities that I think I might have in surgery or decision-making processes are gifts from God. In the long run, I hold these in stewardship, and I am responsibile to Him for the way I use them.

For that reason, I try to integrate what I do in my professional life with what I believe in my Christian life, so that I don't live those two parts of my life in separate compartments.

18

Researching for Longer Youth

"To help people to die as young as possible" seems like a strange ambition for a medical researcher—until he clarifies it, explaining that his goal is to extend youthful vigor into advanced years.

While some of his research colleagues grasp frantically at any drug that may prolong life for even a few months, *Dr. Robert L. Herrmann* finds his Christian faith liberating him from that desperation.

Dr. Herrmann shared his thoughts with RADAS Director Dave Fisher at the American Scientific Affiliation's 1981 annual meeting at Eastern College, in St. David's, Pennsylvania.

Dr. Robert L. Herrmann *received his Ph.D. in biochemistry from Michigan State University. He did postgraduate research at Massachusetts Institute of Technology from 1956 through 1959, first as a Damon Runyan Fellow and then as a Research Associate.*

For seventeen years, Dr. Herrmann taught biochemistry at Boston University's School of Medicine—where he succeeded Isaac Asimov, the prolific writer of more than two hundred books of science and science fiction. In 1976, he moved to Oklahoma to help Oral Roberts University establish its schools of medicine and dentistry. Under his administration, the school staff grew from zero to 47 research scientists and 35 clinical faculty members.

He is a fellow of the American Association for the Advancement of Science (AAAS), the American Scientific Affiliation (ASA), and the Gerontological Society and a member of the American Society of Biological Chemists and the Christian Medical Society (CMS).

Since 1981, Dr. Herrmann has been full-time Executive Director of the American Scientific Affiliation, an organization of approximately 3,000 Christians, all professionally engaged in the sciences. He is also a member of the adjunct faculty of science at Gordon College, in Wenham, Massachusetts.

RADAS: Dr. Herrmann, what makes a person age?

ROBERT HERRMANN: There appears to be an *aging mechanism* in the body. My focus has been on the genetic level—on the idea that there is some basic process of *deterioration* that goes on at the level of DNA, the genetic material within all the cells of the body.

Different cells of the body are replaced at different rates. For example, mucosal cells in the intestinal tract turn over very rapidly, probably within a matter of days. At the other extreme, the neuronal cells in the brain are very seldom replaced.

So we have a more urgent interest in the brain cells. Because they have so little opportunity to regenerate, those are the ones that it's most imperative to protect.

RADAS: Don't people in some places live much longer than the average?

HERRMANN: Yes, the Soviets have one of the three world-noted repositories for old people, in the Caucasus region of the Georgian SSR. Some people there claim a longevity exceeding 120 to 130 years.

There are two other places in the world—in the Andes of Ecuador and in the Himalayas of Nepal—where people can document ages in that range.

From studying those long-lived individuals, we've learned that there is probably a *maximum human lifespan*—seemingly on the order of 120 years. These three areas seem to have a higher proportion of people who live to that maximum age, based on two salient factors.

The first is a low caloric intake. The second is hard physical work in a setting where old people are still considered the family patriarchs—the respected, useful leaders of the clan. Under those conditions, people literally work until they drop dead. They do not atrophy into a vegetative existence.

Some interesting studies have shown how devastating the current social attitude of Western culture has been. Where old people are considered of no value, they simply deteriorate. That seems to lead to a soured attitude and also to some measurable pathology.

RADAS: You've been talking about brain cells. How does aging affect cells in the parts of the body that do regenerate?

HERRMANN: According to present theory, such cells replace themselves with inferior copies of themselves. DNA and RNA control the manufacture of new cells in a way sometimes illustrated by a blueprint analogy.

With time, the genetic "blueprint" becomes fuzzy, or cluttered with debris. Most cells have a certain amount of capacity to repair the error. But certain kinds of damage are less easily repaired, and as an individual grows older, these less reparable insults begin to predominate.

Eventually, there is not enough valid information left to produce a new cell that is in any way functional. At that point, the organism dies.

RADAS: James Watson and Francis Crick won the 1962 Nobel Prize for Medicine or Physiology as a result of their DNA research. They described the normal shape of genetic material as a "double helix," resembling a spiral staircase. Does aging distort that shape in some way?

HERRMANN: Yes. When working with a certain strain of mice, we find that a significant change in the structure of their DNA occurs when the animals begin to look a little scruffy and arthritic.

By the time half of the mice in the experiment have died, many of the survivors show an abnormal, hairpin shape in their DNA, in place of the uniformly-curving helix. We think that signifies that the DNA has undergone some kind of insult that makes it impossible for the DNA to open up and have its information read out in the form of a message.

Therefore, part of the genetic information is buried in the hairpin curvature—of no more use to the organism, because it is no longer accessible.

RADAS: You told a reporter that your object was not to lengthen life itself, as much as to lengthen *useful* life.

HERRMANN: Yes, "to die as young as possible," would be the facetious way to put it, I guess. More seriously, we aim to extend people's health and vitality for many additional years—to try to extend the vigor of those middle years.

Nutrition and exercise are valid considerations in achieving that goal. I think also that we ought to try to recapture a deeper respect and concern in our society for the older members of our population.

RADAS: At lunch the other day, you were joking about researchers consuming a lot of Vitamin E. What's the story on that?

HERRMANN: A lot of work has suggested that some drugs will trap out those substances that cause injuries to DNA and other parts of the cell. Vitamin E has been implicated as possibly useful in that way. I don't think the data are very conclusive, but scientists are human, and some of them feel that they must grab at any straw as their only hope.

Early in the research, one heard in meetings a feeling that it was not even appropriate to talk about prolonging life. It was more a question of how to make the middle years more productive. But now there are people who are openly saying that we can live much longer, and that this is what they are really looking for.

A person who has no comprehension that God is at work in the world has an urgency about living as long as he can—sometimes even a panicky desperation. I don't share that frenzy, because I understand that this life is not all that there is. Instead of the "un-faith" of some of my research colleagues, I have an eternal expectation—a heavenly home that I expect to inhabit for a far longer period than my earthly lifetime. We read that in God's house are many mansions, and Jesus said that He was going to prepare a place for us there.

For me, death is not the grim reaper. My departure will be a time when I will experience some sadness in terms of leaving friends and family, but it will not be the consummation—the ultimate, final defeat—that it is for people who have no faith.

I know I am a part of God's master plan. I am not here by chance or by accident, but by prescription. And my death will be a part of that same plan of a loving God who is ready to promote me to a better world.

In Scripture, Jesus challenged His hearers with the fact that there must be a time in each person's life when he must make a *choice*—either to enter into God's eternal life, or simply to go his own way. The Book of Genesis gives us a preview; Adam and Eve made the choice to "be as gods," to control their own destinies. By that choice, they hid from God and excluded themselves from fellowship with Him.

RADAS: When and how did you make your decision?

HERRMANN: When I was about twelve years old, I was challenged to make a specific decision to commit my life to Jesus Christ. My mother and my father were both devout Christians and lived their lives with an appreciation for God's activity in the world and in their individual lives. So I came very easily to a point of recognizing that this was a viable option.

Since that time, my life has followed—with some ups and downs—a path of seeking to draw my power from the risen Christ, and to try to be God's representative in the world.

I don't think that my decision to follow the God of the Bible was simply a temporal one. God has extended my life more than gerontological research will ever do—in breadth as well as length.

The life God has given me is *infinite*—not only in its eternal duration, but also in its infinite satisfaction through contact with the infinite God.

19

Communicating— with God!

The testimony that follows is unique in this book. It tells the personal experience of *Richard B. Andrews*, a British pioneer of radio. The story is in two parts, written eighteen months apart. The first tells about how Dick met God for the first time; the second, written just before the death of his body, explains how he was able to face that prospect with, as visitors remarked, "a calm and happy spirit."

Dick told us this: "During my life, my chief scientific interest has been in communications, especially radio. I can remember well a schedule I had with a colleague on the other side of the North Atlantic. He and I were testing a new low-powered transmitter/receiver system. Just before the appointed time, I switched on the receiver and began to tune it. Not long after that, I heard his call sign, asking me to 'Come in!'

"I replied and waited.

"He came back.

"We had made contact. We could *communicate!*

"I have enjoyed my life's work—the thrill of communicating with people I knew I would never see, and helping many more to do the same. But how much more thrilling it is to know that, with far less effort, we can communicate with *God*—and be *certain* of successful contact! For I understand that He is always ready to listen to us.

"I do not say that His answers are always those that we expect, but we who trust Him know that whatever His answer it is always right. The most thrilling thing of all to me is that one day I will even 'see Him face to face.'"

Richard B. Andrews *(Dip. Eng., B.Sc., M.I.E.E.) was born in India in 1907. Because of his poor health, he was sent to England one year later.*

When he was still a youth, his interest in electronics had already been awakened. But, at that time, no degrees were offered in that subject.

Later, he proceeded to obtain a degree in electrical engineering from the University of Bristol before joining Standard Telephones and Cables (now part of I.T.T., the international communications company), to work on the development of radio.

In 1950, he was elected a member of the prestigious Institute of Electrical Engineers. During his thirty-eight years with Standard Telephones and Cables, he witnessed the growth of radio from a novel experimental system to an everyday part of twentieth-century life, and the remarkable upsurge of electronics, which has revolutionized the way many things are done.

His interest in RADAS was sparked by his contact with SGA in the capacity of Missionary Secretary of his church, a Brethren Assembly in the village of Martock, in South Somerset, England.

Dick Andrews communicated with God face to face in May 1980, shortly after completing the second part of the following autobiographical account.

While I was at secondary school in England, my French master—a keen radio enthusiast—invited me to listen to his homemade receiver. That was before the British Broadcasting Corporation had been established. We listened instead to one of the earliest transmissions from the Eiffel Tower in Paris. Donning the headphones, I listened with wonder to the crackly strains of Mendelssohn's "Song Without Words."

Little did I realize then that I would have much to do with the development of radio myself. Nor did I know that more than thirty years later I would get a call from a colleague in the Measurements Laboratory of the company for which I worked, inviting me to witness another historic event. That time I listened with amazement to transmissions from the first artificial Earth satellite, Sputnik I, launched the day before, as it crossed over the British Isles.

Born in India in 1907, but sent to England when I was still a baby, I did not really get to know my parents until they came home thirteen long years later. Little did I realize at our reunion how much my life was about to change.

First, I was sent to a new school, which taught science well. I found that change welcome, for I was already interested in science. But second, and even more importantly, my parents were concerned as much with my *spiritual* welfare as with my education. Some years before returning home from India they had become committed Christians. I soon realized that they, and the other members of their church, had something I had not.

In the 1920s, it was fashionable among some groups of people to doubt God's existence. They said that science could explain everything, from the very beginning of the universe! I had been exposed to such philosophy, and it took me some time to realize that, although spiritual and scientific phenomena occupy different spheres, yet they are harmoniously interrelated. Science can teach us about the power of God and the wonders of the universe, for these are evident in the material realm, but it has nothing to say about the nature of God, nor of His relationship with man. Those things are centered in the spiritual realm. I realized that Christians and scientists are both seeking the truth, and neither has anything to fear from the other.

I discovered that many scientists in the world are followers of Christ, and I found that I had little difficulty believing in a Supreme Being. When I looked at the sun, moon, planets, and stars, and considered their diversity and orderly behavior, I had no alternative but to acknowledge that they must all be controlled by some law created by a Supreme Being. There had to be a God.

I grew worried: *Compared to those heavenly bodies, how insignificant is man!* I thought. *Why should God be interested in him? Why should He be interested in me?* Then I discovered this passage in the Psalms: "When I look at the sky, which you have made, at the moon and the stars, which you set in their places—what is man that you think of him; mere man, that you care for him?" (8:3-4, *Good News Bible,* Today's English Version).

I became sure that God does care for us. But even that realization left me feeling very unsettled. There was so much I still did not understand.

The turning point for me came when I heard a talk at church about how Jesus and His disciples were in a boat crossing the Sea of Galilee. Jesus was tired and fell asleep. As He slept, a severe storm arose. Being tossed and buffeted, the disciples—despite the fact that some of them were fishermen and knew the sea—were afraid. They awoke Jesus, and, much to their amazement, *He calmed the storm* (see Matthew 8:23-27).

I knew that, in a spiritual sense, I had been going through a stormy patch, not knowing where to look for guidance and help. I had begun to realize that God loved me and cared for me. I had seen others around me—particularly my parents—who had trusted God, and I had seen how He had changed their lives and had given them peace and contentment. It was a revelation to me to learn that Jesus was God's Son, who had been sent to Earth to demonstrate the power of God—not only over the world of *nature*, but also in the realm of the *spirit*.

I wanted the joy, peace, and contentment that I saw in others. But how could I get in touch with Him? I had communicated with people thousands of miles away—could I communicate with God? Would He forgive me for my doubts? Would He reveal Himself to me?

I decided to try to speak to Him. My prayer was answered; I had got through to God! How I thanked Him for His great salvation!

During my college days, I was much encouraged to meet fellow scientists—professors, engineers, and students—who were Christians. And, subsequently, looking over my whole life, I can honestly say that God has never forsaken me. Indeed, the way He has guided and arranged things has been nothing short of wonderful. Although He has not always planned things the way I myself would have chosen, I have always realized afterwards that His ways were truly right and best.

* * *

After nearly seven years of happy, busy retirement, I experienced what seemed to be a minor setback to my normal good health. Loss of weight prompted me to go to the doctor, who advised an X-ray. But that revealed no serious disorder. Nevertheless, the doctor recommended that I see a specialist.

The specialist, in his turn, ordered more detailed tests, finally suggesting an exploratory operation. He did not hide his concern, nor mask the danger of this step; he made it clear that he feared cancer. However, as my wife and I listened to the possibilities, we were conscious of complete peace of mind and confidence in God, notwithstanding our natural fears.

The operation was carried out. It was as the specialist had feared. The cancer had already spread to several organs. There could be no treatment, and no cure.

At home once again, my wife and I faced the situation with many tears. We had enjoyed nearly thirty-six years of outstandingly happy marriage. The thought of separation seemed unbearable. Yet we were able to encourage each other with reminders of God's promises: He would be our refuge in trouble and our source of strength. So we turned to Him as the only One who could meet us in our great need.

This was the real time of testing of my faith in God. How was all of this to help me in my present situation? Questions assailed me, as though an enemy were attacking me with a hail of arrows.

Why should I have cancer?

Why doesn't God heal me, if He is truly God?

Where is God's love for me now?

Does God care about me and my family in our sorrow?

I was able to withstand the attack and win the battle for three reasons. First, I remembered the many occasions when God had helped me before

in times of difficulty. Second, I read in God's
Word, the Bible, words of reassurance such as:
"When you pass through the waters, I will be
with you" (Isaiah 43:2a); "I am with you always,
even to the end of the age" (Matthew 28:20b);
and, "I will not fail you or forsake you" (Joshua
1:5b). Third, the Holy Spirit, whom God gives
to indwell those who believe in the Lord Jesus,
kept my heart and mind at peace.

As a science graduate at the university, I had
had at my command a fairly good knowledge of
the wonders achieved by science. I had admired
and appreciated them, but, in this crisis, I found
that their cold logic could offer me no comfort.
Although I was certainly grateful for letters from
former colleagues who wrote expressing their
sympathy, I derived little help from those who
conveyed no hope of a life beyond death.

By contrast, my friends who believed in Jesus
Christ reminded me of the Christian's certainty
of eternal life and strengthened my faith in the
loving purposes of God, even through adversity.
Many of them referred to promises that they
themselves had received from God's Word. We
were particularly touched by a note from a friend
whose husband had just died; she quoted:
"Those who *wait for the Lord* will gain new
strength; they will mount up with wings like ea-
gles, they will run and not get tired, they will
walk and not become weary" (Isaiah 40:31, italics
added).

Another gave us this promise: "We know that
in *all things* God works for good with those who

love him" (Romans 8:28, *Good News Bible,* italics added). From many parts of the world I received news of prayers being offered on my behalf.

What, in practical terms, did all of those prayers accomplish? I was not granted a miraculous cure; the disease took its own course through my body. But I thanked God for the aid of medicine, which dulled the pain and enabled me to spend nights of sound sleep. I also thanked God for the support for my Christian family. My daughter returned from her work in Africa to help care for me. My son and his family came to visit me whenever it was possible.

Anyone who has had this kind of illness will know the tendency for the sufferer to become impatient, irritable, and depressed. In those areas of the mind and spirit, medicine can give very little help, but the prayers of many friends brought God's answer. *I found that I could be patient—even cheerful, with my mind at rest—because of my awareness of the presence of God by my side.* Neighbors and others who visited me were, it seems, struck by my calm and happy spirit.

About three months after the exploratory operation, I was still able to get up and dress, and I spent most of my time sitting in my armchair. Each day I spent some time reading my Bible, which, true to God's promise, became more real and living to me as the Holy Spirit opened my mind to its truth. I felt like a miner, extracting treasure from a mine. As my body became more feeble, and my appetite for food decreased, I looked forward ever more keenly to the eternal home promised by the Lord, where sin and pain are forever absent, and endless days are spent joyfully praising and serving Him.

During that period, my greatest desire was to tell others what God had done, especially in dispelling all my doubts and fears. I remembered thinking, years before, "If I am struck down with a fatal illness, will I still have faith in God?" Now that this has happened to me, I am *all the more certain* of God's love and faithfulness! I plead with those who receive this testimony: Put your whole trust in the Lord Jesus, who died and rose again. He, and He alone, can grant eternal life to all who trust in Him. As I did, you should "[cast] *all* your anxiety upon Him, *because He cares for you*" (1 Peter 5:7, italics added).

20

Good Enough for God?

When you walk into a store to buy a product, how can you be certain that the product you purchase will serve you well?

That question is the professional concern of a new branch of engineering, known as "industrial quality control."

Robert Peach has devoted much of his life to consumer protection. His vision for quality control is worldwide—one set of standards for each product everywhere is the ultimate objective.

Robert contends that such a global standard already exists in the spiritual sphere. In the marketplace, the pressure for quality assurance comes from the user, or consumer. In the spiritual realm, however, it is the Maker, or Creator, who demands perfection in His products.

Robert Peach shared something of his testimony, and his view of life in general, with the Dean of RADAS, Dr. Eric Barrett, during SGA week at the Bible and Missionary Conference Center, in Gull Lake, Michigan, in 1981.

Robert Peach *received his B.S. degree from one of the world's most prestigious engineering schools—the Massachusetts Institute of Technology. He followed that with an M.B.A. degree from the University of Chicago. Now head of his own consulting firm, he worked for thirty-three years with Sears, Roebuck and Co., initiating and organizing their Quality Assurance Department during the mid-1950s.*

A Fellow of the American Society for Quality Control (ASQC), Robert is currently a member of the US Delegation to the International Standards Organization, where he is Convenor of the Working Group charged with the preparation of an international standard covering Generic Quality Assurance System Elements.

In 1980, Robert Peach *was honored with the Edwards Medal of the ASQC, in recognition of his lengthy and outstanding contribution to this very specialized field of engineering.*

He is very interested in international Christian missionary work, is board chairman of his church, and has an active involvement in local church planting.

RADAS: Bob, I believe you work in a little-known but vital area of applied science—one that affects almost all of us every day.

ROBERT PEACH: Yes, I do. We all use manufactured items every day, don't we? Most of the time we are satisfied with them. But every so often, we get a nasty shock! Something that we use malfunctions—our television set, for example, or our radio. We are all very annoyed if that happens with an item we have bought only recently—especially if it's not *our* fault that the product has failed us, but clearly the fault of the manufacturer. My work is to try to cut down on the number of problems of that kind.

RADAS: You are a member of the American National Standards Institute and a Fellow of the American Society for Quality Control. Would you explain to us what "quality control systems" are?

PEACH: In order to protect the customer from poor products, it is vital to exercise control over the things that are produced by manufacturing industries. Every product must be able to fulfill its intended purpose. That means that its safety, reliability, and performance must be acceptable to the purchaser. A "quality system" provides an effective and economical means of evaluating any type of product—even, of course, any single manufactured item.

RADAS: That's a most demanding requirement! Tell us about how you came to be involved in this type of work.

PEACH: Surely. I trained first as an engineer at the Massachusetts Institute of Technology. Then I did graduate work in business studies at the University of Chicago. I soon joined a small research group working for Sears, Roebuck, and Company, the largest retailer of general merchandise in the world. Visitors to Chicago soon learn about Sears—the Sears Tower contains the organization's corporate headquarters offices. It is not only the tallest skyscraper in a city that has more than its fair share of them, but it is also the tallest building in the world.

My assignment during my years with Sears was to develop the basis of a scheme that would ensure that products bought by Sears to sell in its stores would meet the standards and specifications that had been set for them. Even then Sears had a huge laboratory for testing such products. My task was to establish the *system* within which laboratory personnel and buyers could do their work most effectively. Such concepts were new in those days, so the work was quite a challenge.

RADAS: What were the most important aspects of the system you developed?

PEACH: I soon found that it was not enough simply to *inspect* the products that had arrived in our warehouses. Most of the manufacturers were highly competent in practical and engineering matters. But many of them did not fully appreciate the quality requirements of the customer.

To our amazement, we found that there was no single set of quality standards to guide the manufacturer and to give assurance of good quality to the customer. So we set out to construct a very formal system to ensure that, day by day and hour by hour, mass-produced products would be good enough to sell to the general public.

RADAS: You must have been very successful! I know that reports prepared under your chairmanship have been accepted by the American National Standards Institute, and that you are now a delegate to the Certification Committee of the International Standards Organization. What is the role of that Committee?

PEACH: Interest in quality systems has been growing in many industrialized countries. Quality systems have been prepared in countries such as Canada, France, Great Britain, and South Africa. My working group was set up by the International Standards Organization to harmonize the several quality systems that have been developed. Our aim is to achieve a single document that will provide one standard for use in all countries of the world.

RADAS: You must be pleased that your pioneering work has been so widely followed! How did you become interested in such an innovative profession?

PEACH: I don't look upon myself as the pioneer in this standards business! When I was a small boy, I first came to realize that *God* had given us a standard to be met by everyone.

The best known form of God's standard for the world is found in the Ten Commandments. Although those guidelines were given thousands of years ago, they are still appropriate today. Indeed, they form the basis of the legal codes in many countries. Many of the commandments are very well known, and they are clearly vital to the smooth running of human society—whether we believe in God or not. "You shall not murder" is one of them. "You shall not steal" and "You shall not commit adultery" are others. When God's Son, Jesus Christ, was alive on Earth, He proved that it was possible to live a perfect life according to those standards.

I was baptized as a Christian believer at the age of ten. Since that time I have tried, with God's help, to satisfy His standards in my life. I guess it was kind of natural for me to go on to apply similarly exacting standards to my work, and to the work of others.

RADAS: Thinking quickly, it would seem that God has not only set *standards* for us to achieve, but also a *"quality system"* to distinguish between good and bad choices of action.

PEACH: Exactly so. What matters in the spiritual realm is *whether or not our lives are acceptable to God.* Jesus Christ is not merely a demonstration of a perfect life—He is also the *pattern* we have to achieve, if we are to enjoy and benefit from God's friendship and help.

In industry, sub-standard products lead first to complaints, and then, if those are sufficiently serious, to rejection of the items. In the same way, God has the right to complain to us about our lives, if they do not reach His very exacting standards. He also has the right to reject us completely, if we do not trust Him alone for personal salvation.

God's standards are so exacting that we cannot achieve them on our own. We need His help. He promises to give aid to any who ask Him to forgive them for their faults and to remake them in the way He chooses and approves. I first asked Him to help me in this way when I was only six or seven years old.

RADAS: How does the Christian believer then discover *in detail* what God's standards are for the rest of his life?

PEACH: He can discover them by reading the Bible. The Bible is the international handbook for God's Quality Control System for men's lives!

Without standards of behavior in a society, we would have anarchy. Without spiritual standards, we are rebelling against God. The Bible tells us all we need to know about the standards that we are, by duty, to achieve. We look to God Himself for the guidance and ability that we need in order to meet them, and so to please Him.

A conscientious manufacturer is always trying to upgrade his product and so to give more and more satisfaction to his customers. I know that, as a Christian, I often disappoint God. But, as all practicing Christians ought to do, I am always making conscious efforts to please God more. The more I try, the more He helps. So, my main aim in life now is to help other people to meet God's spiritual standards too, by discovering His assistance.

21

The Wisdom of Hind-sight

For many years *Dr. Eric C. Barrett* had a problem.

As a university professor, he spent much of his time researching and teaching in the environmental sciences. As one of the pioneers of the everyday application of satellite data in these fields, he has traveled widely for the United Nations and other bodies, advising on such matters as rainfall assessment, pest control, crop prediction, and hazard monitoring, all using satellite data inputs to make life temporarily better for other people.

But as a committed Christian, he was active in church circles, too—first as a lay preacher, and then, from 1967 on, as an Honorary Area Representative for the Slavic Gospel Association. Deputation meetings then took up much of his spare time.

Conscious of the danger that "academic Christians may grow colder by degrees," Eric's inclination was always to try to keep his Christian faith and his work in science reasonably separate. Clearly, he was often unsuccessful. He recalls wryly how, one Monday morning, a meteorology lecture he gave at Bristol University was unexpectedly interrupted by a clear "Amen!"

Recently, Dr. Barrett received the personal challenge from SGA's General Director, Peter Deyneka, Jr., to develop a new science-based radio program, aimed at spreading the gospel of Jesus Christ to the Soviet Union and elsewhere. As a result, it has become obvious to him that God had long planned this much more valuable application of his scientific background and interest.

Today, as Dean of the Radio Academy of Science, and co-editor of this book, Eric Barrett is delighted that he can now combine his science with his knowledge and experience of God to make a *lasting* difference in the lives of others.

Dr. Eric C. Barrett *is Reader in Climatology and Remote Sensing at the University of Bristol, in England. He graduated from the University of Sheffield with a First Class Honors B.Sc. degree in geography in 1962, and an M.Sc. for research in climatic change eighteen months later. He lectured as a full-time member of the staff in the English universities* of Sheffield and Leicester before moving to Bristol in 1965, where he was awarded his Ph.D. in 1969, and a rare "higher doctorate" (the degree of D.Sc.) in 1982 for "his sustained and distinguished contribution to geographic science."

A Fellow of three select scientific societies, he was recently awarded the Hugh Robert Mill Medal and Prize of the Royal Meteorological Society for his research into the estimation of rainfall from satellite cloud imagery.

Following spells at the Australian universities of New England and Western Australia in the late 1960s and early 1970s, he became increasingly interested in the use of satellite remote sensing in developing countries. He has served a number of United Nations bodies as Consultant [UN Disaster Relief Organization and the Food and Agriculture Organization (FAO)], Lecturer (FAO), or Rapporteur (UNESCO). Dr. Barrett is also the United Kingdom's National Representative on the council of the European Association of Remote Sensing Laboratories, and he has current research contracts from the European Space Agency and the US Department of Commerce. He is author or editor of a dozen scientific books, plus about a hundred scientific papers, articles, and reports.

Since 1967, he and his wife, Gillian, have served as Honorary Area Representatives for the Slavic Gospel Association in southern Britain. Today he serves SGA also as Dean of RADAS.

Eric and Gillian are glad to be members of Kensington Baptist Church, in Bristol, England. It is an increasing delight for them to share their Christian ministry with their children, Andrew and Stella.

My life has been dominated by two things: my career in science and my faith in God—despite the common claim that, if science and the Christian faith are not actually incompatible, then they are at least entirely different. In particular, it is often suggested that, whereas the one is logical, the other is beyond logic.

Some Christian scientists have countered such views with the assertion that this alleged dissimilarity is more *apparent* than *real*. They point to undeniable "acts of faith," which many scientists perform in order to "break fresh ground" and to advance beyond current knowledge and understanding. Many new discoveries are made through the exercise of logic, but others result from steps *beyond* logic—practical expressions of the belief that certain things may be true. Many scientists, well accustomed to reaching out through faith in order to explore unknown areas of the material universe, have also found God by reaching out in a similar way into the realm of spiritual reality. They became scientists first, then Christians later.

My own experience was different: I became a scientist long after I had become a Christian. And it is my testimony—after thirty years as a Christian and twenty years as a professional scientist—that there are strong parallels between the practice of science and the practice of the Christian faith. Now, with the wisdom of hindsight, I can see that I followed what we call "the Scientific Method" in my search for God and my subsequent walk with Him—long before I learned about this method and its honored position in science.

Let me explain how it happened.

The *first step* of the Scientific Method involves the *observation* of events and situations. What did I observe that first set me thinking about spiritual things? I was eleven years old at the time. That may be considered a very immature age. However, even then, many children are quite capable of observation, careful thought, and reasoning.

I had served for two years as a choirboy in the Church of England, the "established church" in my country. The Anglican services were very formal and ritualistic. I had observed nothing there to make me think that churchgoers were any different from other people, except for their strange desire to go and spend time in church for no visible reward. As a choirboy I was *paid* (although not very much!) for my attendance at services, practices, and—best of all—weddings. But I could not understand the churchgoers' reason for their attendance.

Then, suddenly, my mother's whole life changed visibly. She herself had never been a regular churchgoer, but she now announced that she had been "converted," through chance attendance at another church that I did not know.

The change in her life was impressive, but I was certain that it would not last. I was nonplussed, though, soon afterwards, when my older sister's behavior also changed. Apparently, the reasons were the same!

To say that I was very puzzled by those developments would be a great understatement. But, after some careful thought, I reckoned that closer study might clarify the issues. So I agreed to miss Evensong one Sunday and go to church with Mother and Sheila. There I took the *second step* in the Scientific Method: I *observed*, and then *analyzed*, what I saw and heard.

What struck me most—in the context of the simple, but obviously sincere, services—was that I heard clearly and directly, for the first time in my life, that man without God is incomplete, and unable to realize his full potential by his own efforts or "good works." I learned that, by himself, man cannot please God—and that eternal separation from God is the penalty for incurring His displeasure. Happily, I also discovered that God has always loved mankind—so much so that He provided, through His own Son, Jesus Christ, both a substitute for my sin and a channel for God's love into my life. It seemed very odd to me at the time that I had never come to such conclusions through years of attendance at my other church!

I looked around at the other people in the congregation. There was no doubt about it: whatever, or *whoever,* had changed two members of my family had clearly changed most of these other folk as well. In general demeanor, they were *all alike*—but different from almost everyone else I knew. I paid careful attention to all that was said and done.

My analysis led me to this simple conclusion: two things were necessary to change me, too. The first was repentance to God for all I had done wrong. Like most other boys of eleven, my conscience was (understandably!) acute—it's not until later in life that a person's conscience becomes very actively suppressed. The second was faith in Jesus Christ as God's Son, the One who was punished in my place at Calvary, and who rose again from the dead to mediate for me before His Father—and mine—in Heaven.

One Sunday, I suddenly felt the urge to progress one step further. I wondered, *Could faith in God really make a difference in me, too?* I could only find out by *experiment*. To my surprise, I found that, as I tried to trust Him, so I could; that very instant I *did* believe in Him!

I was so surprised by the overwhelming sense of God in me and beside me that, at first, I forgot to ask Him to forgive me for years of neglect and disobedience to Him. Then I remembered that was what I had to do. After that, I just had to tell others that *the first experiment of my Christian life had been an incredible success!* Through all the years that have followed, I have still been able to enjoy the feeling of euphoria that I felt as I walked home that summer evening.

There comes a time when a scientist has completed enough observation, analysis, and experimentation to be able to *model* his findings into scientific theories and laws. As I got to know

God better through my teenage years, enjoying many of the activities in the life of my newly-adopted local church, my confidence in the Bible as the Word of God continually grew.

At school, my interests were increasingly focused on the sciences. And, as I appreciated more and more the debt we owe to earlier scientists for bringing us to our present level of knowledge, I determined to use God's textbook, the Bible, as a means of boosting rapidly my understanding of Him. I became interested in the great doctrines of the Christian faith—models of the nature and activity of God, the states and positions of men before and after they trust in Him, and His plans and purposes for the world. And I learned more of the laws of God—His immutable guidelines laid down for the good of everyone to whom He has given life.

For many of my colleagues in the scientific community, the Scientific Method—observation, analysis, experimentation, model building, and development through hypotheses, theories, and laws—is quite sufficient in itself. They see no need to do any more with their science. They are called "pure" scientists.

But some of us see things differently. We are at least as concerned with the use of science in everyday problem-solving as we are with the solving of problems for the sake of advancing scientific knowledge. We are called "applied" scientists.

Of course, it is natural for any scientist to learn the essence of his profession before he can put it to proper use—pure science is the springboard into the pool of applications. So, in my case, my early scientific work was pure, rather than applied. My M.Sc. research represented a purely academic study of the influence of cities on climatic change. And who could find a ready application for my Ph.D. thesis on "The Contribution of Meteorological Satellites to Dynamic Climatology"? It was not until later, from the early 1970s on, that my interests began to change, and my work became much more *practical*.

Again, my experience as a Christian parallels this principle. Pure science pursues knowledge for its own sake. It neither presumes nor seeks uses for its findings: The world of matter is worth exploring for its own sake. The life of the Christian also involves a search. The Bible says that the Christian must "grow in grace, and in the knowledge—and love, of God." For some, that exploration of God is enough.

But, on the other hand, just as we have great scope to apply the findings of science in helping and serving others, so we are commanded by God to share our knowledge of Him with other people. The Bible also says that we are "saved to serve." Anything that the believer learns of God could be of value to his fellow men. So "pure" and "applied" Christianity also go hand in hand.

During my late teen years, I began to accept the challenge—along with the responsibility—of sharing my Christian faith with others. At first, I did this by teaching Sunday school. Then, while I was a student at the University of Sheffield, I became involved in lay preaching and gospel team activities.

When I reached my late twenties, God led my fiancee, Gillian, and me to accept an invitation to become unpaid, spare time representatives of the Slavic Gospel Association. We have served the mission in this capacity from 1967 to the present. Never have I found science difficult to reconcile with my faith and experience as a Christian. As Kepler once put it, science is "thinking the thoughts of God after Him." Oddly, though, until the mid-1970s, I never had any interest in using science itself as a means of helping others more than just physically or mentally.

Then, quite unexpectedly, and in quick succession, I received two invitations to write science-based programs for Christian radio: first from Peter Deyneka, Jr. (now General Director of SGA), and then from Reverend Joseph Steiner (Head of Hungarian Broadcasting at Trans World Radio, in Monte Carlo). Soon after my first successful efforts, I was asked to design and develop a wholly new evangelistic and pre-evangelistic scientific program for SGA, using science as its base. Liking the thrill of a new challenge, I accepted the responsibility.

So, in the summer of 1977, RADAS (The Radio Academy of Science) was hatched. David Fisher joined our staff as Editor in 1979, and, after much effort, this fledgling program took to the air for the first time on January 1, 1980.

Since then, the growth of RADAS has been remarkable. It now includes a whole family of ministries—adult and children's programs in several languages, audiovisual materials, magazine articles, and books (including this collection of testimonies). That's far more than I dared dream about, when I first jotted down preliminary plans on the back of an old airmail envelope in Chicago in 1976!

For me, RADAS has become the answer to an oft-repeated prayer: "Lord, why have You not called me into 'full-time service' for You?" To the Christian 'overtimer,' the single-mindedness of 'full-time service' seems laden with strong, yet unrealizable, allure. Like many Christians in my position, I had long accepted the idea that one answer to my question was that God—for reasons of His own—had not willed that I should serve Him in a direct full-time capacity. How overjoyed I was to discover a second answer to my question: God wants me to use my science, and my status as a scientist, to help win others for Him.

This more complete answer came only after I had been a believer for more than twenty-five years and a professional scientist for more than fifteen. It was then, with the wisdom of hindsight, that I saw this point: whereas full-time Christian service is appointed for some, many kinds of Christian service are reserved for laymen, who—because of their secular skills or positions in society—are better equipped to undertake such tasks successfully. How I wish now that I had had more patience while God was preparing me to fulfill His main purpose for my life. But He is the only One who sees the end from the beginning. Only He knows the future.

This mention of the future brings me to my last consideration.

Perhaps the *final goal*—and *the toughest test*—of science is found in the *prediction of the future*. Scientists say this: "If we have the data we need, and we understand a type of situation well enough, we must be able to predict the outcome of related experiments or natural events."

As a Christian, I have *data* on the spiritual situation in the world today: there are many people who do not know God for themselves. And I *understand* that He remains the Lord of life. So, not surprisingly, my firm prediction—and that of Scripture—is that the day is coming when God will say to each of us, "Enough! Give Me an account of all that you have—or have not—done!"

It is in this crucial area that the parallels I see between science and the Christian faith break down. I often remark to my students (to keep us all humble) that as scientists, we do the things we do today so that someone else may be able to do them better tomorrow. But, as a Christian, I know that there are things God wants *me* to do that can never be done by another person. He holds me personally responsible for those. Furthermore, there may be *no tomorrow* in which I can do those things if I fail to do them today.

What must our conclusion be? Except for key areas, which embrace the role and responsibility of the individual, science and Christianity are so compatible that they can both be approached by a common method. Its hub is *experimentation*— the testing, in faith, of an initial notion or hypothesis. And, as such, the experiment with

Christianity is something every one of us can perform, whether our training lies in science or any other field.

The Bible puts it like this: *"Taste* and *see* that the Lord is good" (Psalm 34:8*a*, italics added).

Every contributor to this book has obeyed that command and put the dependent promise to a successful test.

Have you?

Appendixes

1. THE SLAVIC GOSPEL ASSOCIATION

SGA is a global, non-denominational, evangelical missionary society whose aim is "To reach with the gospel of Jesus Christ, the three hundred million Slavic-speaking peoples, and others, as the Lord directs." It was founded in 1934 by Peter Deyneka, a Russian emigrant with a deep concern for the spiritual well-being of his compatriots.

Today, SGA has its headquarters in Wheaton, Illinois, under the direction of Peter Deyneka, Jr. It supports some 260 full-time workers, and assists many national workers behind the Iron Curtain. Its chief ministries are in radio, literature, evangelism, refugee relief work, church planting, and support.

2. THE RADIO ACADEMY OF SCIENCE

RADAS is a growing group of integrated projects using science as a vehicle for evangelistic and pre-evangelistic ministries. Beginning in January 1980, as a weekly thirty-minute radio program in Russian, the parent program is now broadcast to the Soviet Union some fifteen times each week from eight international Christian radio stations. At present, it is also translated for use in several additional languages. The first English-language transmissions were made in collaboration with Trans World Radio and HCJB.

Some of the program's contents are reprinted in Christian magazines in Eastern Europe. Audiovisuals are also being prepared for use in East European churches. In March 1982, the adult RADAS program was joined on the air by a "junior RADAS" under the title of "Nature World." These ministries depend heavily on materials supplied by Christians around the world who are active in scientific pursuits.

3. SOME USEFUL ADDRESSES

If you have found this book helpful, or if you would like to learn more about the Slavic Gospel Association, mail your letters to:

>   Slavic Gospel Association
>   P. O. Box 1122
>   Wheaton, Illinois 60189 USA

Or to one of SGA's international offices:
Av. Meeks 860
Temperley 1834
Buenos Aires, Argentina

P. O. Box 216
Box Hill
Victoria 3128, Australia

P. O. Box 280
Paget, Bermuda

37a The Goffs
Eastbourne
East Sussex BN21 1 HF
Great Britain

P. O. Box 2, Station K
Toronto, Ontario M4P 2G1
Canada

P.O. Box 31337
Auckland, New Zealand

If you would like to learn more about the Radio Academy of Science, or if you live in North America and believe that you have insights or experiences that might be used in RADAS programs, mail your inquiries to:

Mr. David Fisher
RADAS Faculty Office
P. O. Box 1122
Wheaton, Illinois 60189 USA

If you live outside North America and believe that you have insights or experiences that might be used in RADAS programs, mail your inquiries to:

Dr. Eric C. Barrett
The White House
44, Hilldale Road
Backwell, Avon BS19 3JZ UK